Screenwriting
from the Soul

Screenwriting from the Soul

Letters to an Aspiring Screenwriter

Richard W. Krevolin

RENAISSANCE BOOKS

Los Angeles

Library of Congress Cataloging-in-Publication Data

Krevolin, Richard W.
    Screenwriting from the soul : letters to an aspiring screen-
writer / Richard W. Krevolin.
        p. cm.
    Filmography: p.
    Includes bibliographical references and index.
    ISBN 1-58063-036-7 (alk. paper)
    1. Motion picture authorship. 2. Television authorship.
I. Title.
PN1996.K72   1998
    808.2'3—dc21   98-33583
                                                    CIP

10 9 8 7 6 5 4 3 2 1

Design by Joel Friedlander

Distributed by St. Martin's Press
Manufactured in the United States of America
First Edition

Contents

Foreword

The first thing I noticed when I met Rich Krevolin was that he had a pretty girlfriend. Right away I knew he was an authority on movies—or, as they refer to it at USC where he teaches, the Cinema. This happened in the lobby of a hotel near Northwestern University, where we were booked to speak at the same conference. During that weekend we got to know each other better and at a dinner put on by the conference sponsor, we sat together and Rich told me about a book he was writing and how it was going to be based on Rilke's *Letters to a Young Poet*—which led to the next thing I noticed about Rich, that I felt comfortable enough with him to admit that I didn't really know anything about Rilke except that I was supposed to nod my head knowingly whenever I heard his name.

So Rich told me about the book. His book, and Rilke's, and I'm happy to say that my little life is better for having read them both. Because both are saying, essentially, the same thing: that it's how you live your life that matters, and in the living of your life it's how you approach your work and your place as an observer of the world around you, and the responsibilities of that, that will determine your level of happiness and fulfillment—and that all that has to come before you get any professional results. Because if it doesn't, you might not get them—or worse, you might get everything you dreamed about, but blow it by not being "ready."

So what I see this as, is a book about getting ready. And as such, it fills a gap in the current array of books about screenwriting, most of which are often quite useful and occasionally even profound. But even in a niche market there is more than one niche. And while the aspects of screenwriting that I will call, for the sake of this foreword, the "technical stuff," are well covered and available on your bookshelves today, what I don't see covered, at least thoroughly, is what I'll call, again for the sake of this foreword, the "emotional stuff." And that's what makes Rich's book a timely and worthy addition to your shelf.

A word about screenwriting books in general: at a different conference, in Texas, I was on a panel with some really hot writers. I mean, people whose work anybody would respect, people who'd gotten it all, in terms of what you can get when you really ring the bell in this game. And the question came up, as it often does, about screenwriting courses and books, and whether this or any kind of writing can be learned that way at all.

The first writer who answered stuck his thumb right out, turned it down and made a Bronx cheer sort of noise to underscore his feelings on the subject. Now this was a guy who had just won an Academy Award and had a very pretty girlfriend, so he obviously was an expert whose opinion should be heavily weighed.

When my turn came I said I wasn't so sure. However, I haven't won my Oscar yet, I've only been nominated—plus I'm married, happily, to a girl I've known since I was sixteen and am therefore out of the market for pretty girlfriends. So in my case, not being as much of an expert, I thought that not only were screenwriting books a generally good thing, but certain specific ones, if come upon at the right time, could really make a difference, to anyone who doesn't have the writer's version of perfect pitch—and maybe even to those who do. In other words, even if you fly by instinct it's nice to have a map around.

My point here is that it's not so much who you listen to as it is who's doing the listening. And that's what this book deals with. Yes, there's how to write your screenplay—but there's also how to be the person who's doing the writing. There's how to deal with the day-to-day things that are going to happen to you, to me, to us—to every writer, during the different and very distinct stages of this wonderful and maddening process. Because from soup to nuts, there is something completely elevating and something completely ridiculous about every step of the game. And you're going to find it very helpful to have the guiding hand, like Rilke's young friend did, of someone who knows the territory.

For instance, get this: a foreword like the one you're reading is virtually the only thing I can write as a screenwriting professional that (I'm pretty sure) won't get re-written by some other screenwriting professional—or a committee of them—at the whim or caprice of someone else who decides, for whatever reason, that "we need a fresh approach." I mean, even if they (the editors of this book) take out all the parts about pretty girlfriends (which they shouldn't), all that means is that I've been edited. Not replaced, summarily or otherwise, not booted off, paid off, or told to screw off just, simply, "edited."

So if you like the sound of "edited" more than you like the sound of "fired," then maybe you should consider writing books and not movies. But if it's going to be movies then you'd better know, going in, that no matter who you are and how high you rise, this kind of thing can happen. In fact it's likely. And it hurts. And you need to find a way to get up in the morning and write your next day's pages anyway. Because you're a screenwriter now, and that's what screenwriters do.

One more thing about that conference in Texas. When I got off the panel, I was talking to one of the organizers. We were looking up at the stage, at the seven empty chairs where we had all just been sitting, and I was telling her how amazed I was, and how lucky and grateful I felt, to have accomplished enough to be included in a group of people like that. The organizer said the thing that struck her, was that "every single one of them is miserable." That knocked me out. I said, "I'm not miserable. I'm really happy." She said, "Then you're the only one."

In other words, these guys goofed (and yes they were all guys—but women writers goof too). For all their talent and all their hard-earned glory, they really truly goofed if they can sit up there in a jam-packed roomful of admirers and still be miserable. The work is too bleeping hard and the road is too bleeping long to have anybody finally get there, and in the words of the Sundance Kid (via William Goldman), "find out it stinks."

Because it doesn't stink. It shouldn't stink. Parts of it will, but if the whole thing does then you did something wrong—and what a good thing it would be to avoid that. What a good thing it would be to sit in a chair like that one day, have all your success and like it too. And what a good thing it would be to have a book that could help you do that.

So here you go. Turn the page and meet Rich Krevolin—a professor at a place where movies are still Cinema, and where people had damn well better know who Rilke is before they graduate, or at least before they turn forty, which is how long it took me.

Let Prof. K. walk you through the woods on a subject he knows a lot about. And—pretty girlfriend (or boyfriend) (or whatever) or not—may a wonderful career and a happy fulfilling life be the result.

—Jeff Arch, Academy-award nominated screenwriter for *Sleepless in Seattle*

Acknowledgments

This book is dedicated to all my teachers: Mrs. Schapiro, Mr. Parmelee, Ms. Smith, Mrs. Knapp, Mrs. D'Addio, Mrs. Sweetzer, Mr. Lieberman, Mr. Goorhigian, Mr. Hunt, Ms. Crosby, Mr. Guzze, Mr. Garofalo, Mr. Gibbons, Mr. Bonomi, Ms. Flaherty, Mr. Profitt, Mr. Oliver, Master T., Bennett Cohen, Edit Villarreal, and all my other teachers, too numerous to name, at Gan Hayeled Nursery School, Beecher Road School, Amity Junior High School (Bethany), Amity Senior High School, Yale, UCLA, and USC.

Special thanks to—(in alphabetical order):

Hal Ackerman for the prototype scenogram and the mentoring,

Jeff Arch for helping me find the blessings amid all the apparent curses,

Joe Bologna and Sammy Shore for the King,

David Chisholm for the script mentoring,

Big Red Courtmanche, Betsy and T. for believing,

Laura and Mike Cox for my home away from home in OKC,

Meri Danquah for the book world knowledge,

Dawn, Catherine, Betty, Michael, Big Al, and all the Oklahoma Playpens for bringing me back again and again to teach,

Charlie Donato, Esq., for the legal genius (as well as the whole law office gang—Sandy, Sharon, Paula, and Diane),

Bill Hartley, my publisher, for his vision,

Michael J. Dougherty, Debbie Appel, and Kathryn Mills for the marketing support,

John Drdek for good old Dr. Grader,

John Furia for giving me the chance to teach at USC,

Steve Hetherington for the Golden Corral,

Ann Hilborn and the Houston Screenwriter's Group at Mary Ann Mabray's house for always believing in the letters,

Stuey Jaeger, CPA extraordinaire, and Jay Shanker, lawyer extraordinaire, for being essential parts of Team Krev,

Prof. Rick Jewell and Dean Elizabeth Daley for permission,

David Klass for the urging forward through the darkness,

Jon and Rob Krevolin for the brotherly love,

Sherman and Evelyn Krevolin for being the best parents anyone could ever ask for,

J. Michael Legat for the weed whacker scene,

Greg Lemkin, Marc Rashba, Simone Lazer, Dean Chadwin, Janie Larson, Kim Orchen, Claudette Sutherland, Chip Rosenbloom, Marc Olin, Dave O'Brien, Wendy Iscove, Paul Linke, Nanci and Steve Ellis for the kindness and friendship,

Murray, Marvin, and Joyce Lender for giving me love, support, and much more than just bagels,

Steve and Meera Lester (The Writers' Connection) for starting it all at "Selling to Hollywood" in Glendale,

Julie MacClusky for all the teaching gigs,

Barbara Mandel at ICM for believing in my screenplays,

Joanna Miles and the Playwright's Group for the readings,

Paula Munier Lee for starting the ball rolling,

Kerstin Meyer for the early read and enthusiasm,

Bob "Coach of the Year, Mr. Ansonia" Orgovan, Pete Madden, Coach Melonhead "Thom" Jacobs, Chris Dickerson, and Kevin "Guitarman" Ruane for the friendship, support and long runs,

Jim Parish, my editor, for seeing the dream, and Robin Cantor-Cooke for helping make it a reality,

Colleen Sell for believing and praising,

John and Ruth Rauch and the Center for Jewish Culture and Creativity,

Shana for the Sauna, the Tao of Po, editing, loving, supporting, and listening,

John Shubert for the partnership,

Jeff "The Wizard" Rosner for the profound, the stimulating, and the pedestrian running commentary,

Richard Walter, Dr. James Ragan, John Rechy, Ben Masselink, Ron Gottesman, Arnold Margolin, Stirling Silliphant, Cynthia Whitcomb, T. C. (T-Bone) Boyle, David St. John, and David Scott Milton for the inspirational teaching, guidance, and anything which I may have subconsciously borrowed,

Cynthia Weyand for the reunion,

Jimmy Wolf for the summer employment,

Suzanna Zepeda for singing dolphin love songs,

And any and all of my students at USC and around the country who have touched me, believed in my message, and told me I should write this book . . .

Thank you all and God bless.

I came to myself within a dark wood,
where the straight way was lost.

—Dante Alighieri, *The Divine Comedy*

Sullivan: I want this picture to be a document. I wanna hold a mirror up to life. I want this to be a picture of dignity . . . A true canvas of the suffering of humanity.
Lebrand: But with a little sex.
Sullivan: With a little sex in it.

—Preston Sturges, *Sullivan's Travels*

If the fool persists in his folly, he shall become wise.

—William Blake

Letters to an Aspiring Screenwriter

6/11/98

Dear Professor Krevolin:

I am an aspiring writer in need of help. I have always loved films (especially the old ones written by you), and I know I can write movies that are better than the crap that Hollywood seems to be producing these days. I would love to go to USC Film School, but I am really in no position to just get up, move to California, and go to school full time right now. Especially with all the family and job related stuff I'm dealing with right now. I'm sure you can appreciate my situation.

So here's the thing—I heard that sometimes professors consult and I was wondering what your fees are like. I don't have a lot of money, but what little money I do have, I'd be happy to give to you if you could help make me into a real writer.

Please say yes.

Sincerely Yours,

Aspiring

P.S. I have included a copy of my most recent screenplay, *Convertible Man*, which I was hoping you might be able to peruse at your earliest convenience.

P.P.S. Do you have e-mail?

6/20/98

Dear Aspiring:

1. I don't want your dirty money;
2. Keep aspiring;
3. I have taken your screenplay, *Convertible Man*, and tossed it into the cobalt blue Pacific Ocean where it belongs.

Best,

Prof. K.

P.S. No one can make someone into a "real writer." You are either born with the curse or not. The reasons why God chooses to whisper into the ear of one man and not another are known only to him.

P.P.S. E-what? No, I don't believe in computers. I write real letters. By hand. With number two pencils on yellow legal paper. Then I type them out on an IBM Selectric typewriter.

6/26/98

Dear Prof. K.:

You have a lot of nerve. I spent a year writing that script and twelve dollars at Kinko's to copy and bind it and then three dollars to send it to you. Thus, you now owe me fifteen dollars. I expect your check in the mail *ASAP.*

You know, I heard a lot of people say that you were a washed-up, egomaniacal, self-indulgent hack, but I always stood up for you and said that you were just overly sensitive. That is, until now!

Angry and Aspiring

7/6/98

Dear Angry:

I am not a hack. Washed-up? Sure. I scrub my pits with anti-bacterial soap on a daily basis. Egomaniacal? Maybe, but I'm too wrapped up in myself to know for sure. Self-indulgent? Definitely, all writers are, but don't call me a hack. I write for myself and only for myself. I have no desire to try to make money off the struggles of aspiring screenwriters who already have enough financial burden trying to stay afloat in a culture that does not foster creativity. Sorry, but I know there are people all over the country who make a living consulting and would be happy to take your filthy lucre. Trust me, you'll be better off without me.

Sincerely,

Oedipus Wrecks

P.S. There is an ancient proverb that states, "Those who know, do not speak; and those who speak, do not know." So be careful whom you hire as your mentor.

7/15/98

Dear Oedi:

I wrote to you because I'm a fan of your work and I thought of us as kindred spirits who shared a special love of language and literature. But obviously, you don't care for literature anymore as indicated by the fact that you no longer write but instead hole yourself up in an ivory tower to subsidize your lack of a viable writing career. Your refusal to continue to write is a personal decision I can respect, but to be honest, I must tell you that I am truly disappointed that I will have to suffer through the rest of my life without even the hope that I will ever get to read any more of your brilliant work.

In terms of your prospective tutelage, I'm sorry you can't help, but even if you could, the more I get to know you, the more I feel that, even though I love your writing, you may not be the best person for me to work with.

Sincerely,

Disillusioned

P.S. By the way, there's a very good chance that I'll be joining an online writing tutorial program through the UCLA Extension Program. So there!

7/25/98

Dear Di:

Hark, did I touch a nerve? Well, film and theater are visceral, not intellectual mediums, so at least you've got some of the right raw materials. But before you go running off to the enemy (those hairy UCLA Bruins), in the best Socratic tradition, let me answer your question with another question; the first and single most important one that any writer must ask himself . . .

Why write?

Why do some insist upon writing even though they know it will lead them to drink, divorce, or even insanity? Why try to become a screenwriter? Why bother when it's just so much easier to watch TV or go to the movies? *Why write?*

One might as well ask, why breathe? We write because we can't help ourselves; writing keeps us from killing ourselves or others. And deep down in our souls, we write because we yearn to etch one tiny, seemingly insignificant scratch into the stainless steel bones of culture; we fight, we persist, we persevere, we write; we are drawn to language like a junkie to his smack, a baby to her mother's breast, Romeo to Juliet. Throughout history, we find examples of this deeply human need to write, to record, to spin yarns, to create stories; and what better way to have your story told than in magnificent Technicolor on a huge silver screen with booming Dolby THX sound!

For example, take a pale, lonely Czech bureaucrat by the name of Franz Kafka. Kafka spent his life writing and in his last will and testament begged the executor of his estate, Max Brod, to burn all of his work. Now, here's the rub: why didn't Kafka ensure that his work would never be seen by burning it himself? The answer is simply this: As much as Kafka believed his writing to be worthless, there was something deep inside his soul that kept him from lighting the match, something that desperately wanted to believe that maybe, just maybe, what he said might resonate with one person out there who was feeling the same pangs of terror and alienation that Kafka experienced on a daily basis. But mostly, Kafka couldn't help himself. He was a writer. No matter how inferior he believed his work to be, he kept on writing. He wrote for himself; the tragic irony of his life is that he found his terrified and alienated audience only after his death.

The truth is that most of us, like Kafka, are plagued with self-doubt. So, how do we go about discovering if what we write is any good, especially if we don't already have an established agent or producer who will read it? How can we find out if our words speak to others, if our work is not just the self-indulgent spouting of an ego yearning to be recognized, coddled, and loved?

Let me answer this question with a story . . .

A tale is told of a young man who wanted to study Zen Buddhism. He went to the door of the greatest living Zen master and entreated him to take him on as a student. The master slammed the door in his face. The student was resolute and remained through the rainy night, sleeping against the door. The following morning, he knocked once again at the master's door, and once again, he was refused.

All the next week this went on. Each day the student offered the master money, food, and anything of value he could find, but with each offer, he was met only with more rejection. Finally, the student cut off his hand and left it at the master's door. When the master saw the student's steely resolve and bloody stump, he finally agreed to take him on as a student.

So then, in the end, there is no quick fix or final word. Writers prove themselves by doing one thing: they keep on writing. Professional writers spend a great deal of time trying to please others, but when you are starting out, write what you need and want to say. Being a writer is hard, being a professional writer is even harder, and being a working Hollywood screenwriter may be the hardest of all. But if you love stories, if you really, really love them, and more than anything else in the world, you want to write them, well then, just maybe you have IT and this letter will, like the Muse, whisper in your ear, guide your fingers along the keyboard, and fill your mind with fresh characters and ideas.

Sincerely yours,

Master Socrates

P.S. Are you ambidextrous?

P.P.S. In Burma, there are people who make a living catching king cobras. However, sometimes when these fellas are trying to do their job, the snakes take offense and strike them in the head. Now, the only way to stem the flow of the poison is to tie a tourniquet around the affected area (the neck). Obviously, this presents a problem. So, it is said, there is only one recourse. The victim should go find the shade of a tree, sit down, and die like a man.

8/3/98

Dear Master So-So-crates:

Oh, I bet you'd love for me to camp out on your doorstep, do a little self-vivisection, and die like a man. Well forget it, tough guy! You know, right after I finished reading your letter, I was going to write back and tell you that you are a sick, pretentious man, but I decided against that and settled upon telling you a little tale of my own.

There once was a woman who wanted to be a dancer more than anything else in the world. From the time she could first walk, she went to dance classes. When she was eighteen, her boyfriend asked her to marry him. She knew in her heart that if she got married, her dance career and her dreams would be abruptly halted, so she came up with a plan. A famous dance company was coming to town that weekend. She went to see the artistic director and begged him to audition her. He agreed, and after watching her for ten seconds, he shook his head and said, "Sorry, but I don't think you have what it takes." With tears in her eyes, she bowed politely and exited through the back door. That summer, she got married and soon was pregnant. As you may have guessed, she never danced again.

However, years later, when her children were all grown, she read that the same dance company was coming to town once again and so, without her husband knowing about it, she went to see the show. When it was over, she snuck backstage and found the artistic director of the company, who was now very old. She approached him and said, "I'm sure you don't remember me, but more than twenty years ago, your company came to town and I auditioned for you and within a few seconds, you knew I didn't have it."

"Yes. So?"

"Well, my whole life I've always wanted to find out—how did you know so quickly?"

"Honey, if you let one person watch you dance for five seconds, and convince you that you don't have it—well then, you really don't have it!"

Most Sincerely Yours,

Twinkle Toes

P.S. So you see, I believe that I have IT and I can translate IT into a screenplay which I can sell for a lot of filthy lucre and become famous . . . or should I just bag it all and go to business school?

P.P.S. I've decided not to pursue the UCLA thing.

8/11/98

Dearest Twink:

Everyone has a story to tell. But being able to tell it well, to write it down in such a way that others want to pay you for the privilege of seeing it on the big screen, is indeed a rare occurrence. Writing well and structuring your story into an appealing and captivating form is a craft, one that can and should be honed over a period of years. Yes, I would be lying if I said that after reading a few lousy letters, you could write a commercially viable Hollywood script in just twenty-one days. Sure, some pros might be able to do that, but even for most Hollywood insiders, screenwriting is hell and not a short-term stop, but a long, drawn out one.

The development of your own particular voice is a long-term process, but the years of work need not be a hardship, for they can be tremendously rewarding. But if you're entering the writing game for fame and money (filthy lucre?), get out quick. Begone! Shoo! Take your stable income, your mortgage, your medical/dental plan, and scamper off to business school where you belong. Because there are positions all over the globe for well-trained businessmen, and other service professionals, but there are only seven people in the entire freaking world who support themselves as full-time screenwriters. Okay, maybe seventeen, but still . . .

The thing is—every buffoon and his mother was trained to write in elementary school, so everyone believes that they can become a writer in their spare time. Believe it or not, it's the number one hobby in America. So be forewarned. The competition is fierce, and there will be many roadblocks ahead.

However, if you are one of the possessed ones, if you love movies so much you'd rather sit *alone* in a dark movie house than watch the Super Bowl or the Academy Awards on TV (I know this sounds un-American, and for that, I am sorry), then yes, you should be writing screenplays. So, as soon as you finish reading this letter, write ten more screenplays and then throw them all into the ocean to rest in peace next to *Convertible Man*. You see, most fish can't walk over to the local library to find their favorite reading material. They are stuck with what floats by. And thus, tossing overboard your *oeuvre* is a community service of oceanic proportions.

But you argue, "Why should I toss it into the ocean? Why shouldn't I submit it?" Well, because the truth is that until you have written a few screenplays, you probably aren't ready to submit your work, especially to industry professionals. But you argue, "Yes, it's my first screenplay, and it's not *Citizen Kane*, but it's still a whole heck of a lot better than most of the crap that seems to be coming out of Hollywood these days."

I agree with what you said in your earlier letter that most of what Hollywood is producing these days is not very impressive; in fact, it seems as if the occasional well-written Hollywood film is more of a fluke than a commonplace occurrence. However, we must never forget that Hollywood's purpose is not to produce edifying pieces of art and never has been. Hence, it is called show *business*, not show *art*. If you want beauty, go to cosmetology school.

So, I urge you now, before we delve into the dark heart of the screenwriting beast, if you can do anything else, do it. Please! Marry. Procreate. Get divorced. Attain financial security. Buy a suburban sports utility vehicle. The whole schmeer. And enjoy it, because if you can be happy with these things, you are one of the lucky ones. Have a nice life and God bless you.

Good riddance,

The Nay-sayer

P.S. If you spent half as much time and energy on your writing as you did on your letters, who knows what you might achieve? So stop writing to me and start writing poignant, thought-provoking screenplays that come from your heart. And don't ever let anyone tell you that you can only write what you know. You can write anything you want as long as you write what you feel—from a deep, true place inside your soul.

8/19/98

Dearest Nay-sayer of the Apocalypse:

Whoa! I knew you were a bitter, jaded, cynical has-been, but I never dreamed you would have the nerve to try to turn me into a McDonald's employee. So let me just say up front, you are right; if I could go to business school, I would. But I want, I need, I have to write, and after having read your work, I have decided that you are the one who is going to teach me, whether you want to or not.

As one of your beloved Zen monks once said, "When the student is ready, the teacher shall appear and when the teacher is ready, the student shall appear."

So baby, here I am. Work with me!

Excited to learn,

Your most promising two-handed student

9/5/98

Dear Two-Handed Excited Young Thing:

No.

Good luck finding your Zen master,

Your favorite bitter, jaded, cynical, has-been HACK.

P.S. Don't make me have to get a restraining order.

9/10/98

Dear bitter, jaded, cynical, has-been HACK:

I ain't going away. Deal with it.

Persistently yours,

Your little Ray of Sunshine.

P.S. By the way, did I mention that I went to a used bookstore that does searches for out-of-print books and I've compiled a small library of all your old stage plays. Also, I sold my body to the night to raise the money to purchase copies of all your old screenplays. I think they're all marvelous. Tony and Oscar material. It's a shame you were overlooked. You should have had a better PR agent. You know, I tell all my friends that you are the Van Gogh of your day, but with both ears.

And as a result, the tragedy of your extended inactivity looms even larger. So if someone of your talent and gifts has stopped writing, I feel that there must be a reason. What is it? Talk to me. Do older artists just run out of material and dry up, like a riverbed in a drought? I don't want this to happen to me, so please tell me how I can budget my inspiration, you know, so I'll have enough creative fire to last a lifetime. I'm not trying to get too personal, I just want to keep what happened to you from happening to me. If you respond honestly, I promise I'll leave you alone. And I swear, it's all off the record. I'm not a reporter or, God forbid, a tabloid journalist.

9/19/98

Dearest Sunny Ray:

I like it here in the dark. And don't bother knocking on my door, because there's no one home.

Sammy Davis Coleridge Jr.

P.S. If you ever call me a has-been again, I will send out my foot soldiers to destroy you. I can still write. I just have chosen not to. See J. D. Salinger for further explanation.

10/8/98

Dear Sammy:

I love your rocking version of "Rime of the Ancient Mariner." It really swings.

But seriously, if you don't want to teach me, fine—this will be my last letter. But before I sign off, let me just say thank you for sharing your writing with the world. Yes, it has made a difference, at least in my life, and that is why I so desperately want to work with you. But if you are not up to it, I understand.

I remain,

Your biggest fan

P.S. More specifically, since we are never going to correspond again, I thought you should know that a few years ago I read a tattered, dog-eared copy of your play, *Boychik*, which I bought for a nickel at a garage sale. It affected me so deeply that I sent my father a copy, he read it, called me up, and we spoke for the first time in many years. I know that my personal life is probably of no concern to you, but your writing brought me closer to my dad before he died and that is why I am forever indebted to you.

So, whatever your choice, I understand your desire for privacy and will respect your wishes.

11/17/98

Dear Biggest Fan:

A nickel? Even in piss-poor condition, my play's a collector's item worth at least twenty bucks. You've obviously got a good head for bargains.

You know, I had no idea that anyone out there really cared about my work, let alone that it has effected such dramatic, positive change in the lives of others. Thank you for sharing your story with me; it means far more to me than you could ever imagine. I am moved by your passion and will reconsider your proposition. In other words, so-o-o, where do you want to start? With loving affection,

Your hero,

Euripedes Jr., Dramatic Writing God

P.S. As to your recent inquiry as to the reason why I no longer write, the answer stems from professional and personal issues that I do not care to share with you—a stranger—or for that matter, with anyone. Such is life. So, if you want to learn, I'll teach; but please, let us keep my private life out of the mix. Thank you very much.

P.P.S. As to your desire to achieve fame and fortune, I cannot help you. But if you want to achieve greatness, i.e., literary immortality, Arnold Ludwig in *The Price of Greatness: Resolving the Creativity and Madness Controversy*, states that a "template for greatness exists that predisposes individuals to exceptional creative achievement. The key elements of this template include an innate ability or precociousness tempered by suitable education and training, the right kind of parents and family resources, a certain irreverence towards authority, self-sufficiency and independence, a sense of physical vulnerability, the existence of psychological unease, works that bear a personal seal, and a striving for dominance or power."

And from what I've seen from you so far, it appears as if you may in fact have what it takes. So, c'mon, let's go get 'em, Bucko!

11/20/98

Dear Rippy, the Dramatic Writing Machine:

I understand and will respect your desire for privacy.
Okay then, let us start at the beginning, you know, with the fundamentals, and then go from there, okay?

Eagerly Awaiting the Education of my Life,

Your numero uno acolyte

P.S. The template for greatness you presented looks shockingly similar to my personality profile. Wow! Am I destined to be immortal, or what?

1/2/99

Dearest Uno:

Here we go . . .

I have culled my many years of lecture notes and come up with this. Hope it suffices.

So now, let us start all over again with the mother of all questions, *Why write?*

This is a question of self-awareness. Who are you? What are you trying to achieve? What do you really want? What is this primitive need you have to record your thoughts, to tell your stories and to try to convey your dreams and desires, your personal experiences? What do you hope to gain by writing? Do you write to woo, to shame, record, impress, flirt, hurt, thrill? Do you write to damage, to pass the time, plumb the soul, narcotize, stimulate, transcend death, time, space? Do you write to create a thing of beauty, to become immortal? Why does anyone sit alone for hours on end in front of a phosphorescent screen, plastic keyboard balanced precariously upon their thighs, while they smear their blood and bile across the screen?

More specifically, why write movies? What I want you to see from the very beginning is that this is far more than a journey of learning a few screenwriting techniques, this is a journey of self-knowledge; the act of writing a screenplay is merely the crucible in which you will be tested. You must never lose sight of this; the journey is far longer than it seems; there are many more revisions to be done than you can ever imagine. In fact, the path never ends, and even when we fade out and the movie ends, there are always sequels to write. After all the work we do together, I hope you will come to see that what it's all about is not a sale, but the development of your characters' arcs as well as your own character. The path is the goal; the act of creation is significant and valuable in and of itself, and personal fulfillment and happiness, the by-products of all of your creative endeavors.

Let us look for an answer in a fairly recent Hollywood comedy, *Mrs. Doubtfire.* Seventy-nine minutes into this movie (I'm sorry, I time movies, it's my job), Daniel, the main character, played by Robin Williams, is forced to deal with the many complications that result from him trying to lead a dual life and then, in despair, screams out to the world, "What am I doing here? This is *beyond obsession!*"

And so, yes, as you may have already guessed, this is where I want to start: with obsession, and I'm not talking about cologne. Nor am I talking about mere ordinary obsession. I'm talking about being beyond obsession, for this is the only mind-set which will serve as a foundation for a person who wants to be a working writer in a world that is not designed to foster artistic growth and change, but only to inculcate stereotypical sameness and perpetual mass consumption. So then, once you are ready to live a life beyond obsession, you're ready to begin your Hollywood education and, one day, you may even sell something you have written. And then years after your death, like Kafka, you may even achieve a modicum of fame. Maybe . . . But remember: In the end, one writes stories to learn, to further one's own growth as a human being. That is all.

: Stories and Culture

Everything begins with the impulse to tell a story. This is not a luxury, but an essential part of our genetic makeup. We need stories. They give us a context; they locate us within ourselves, our society, and our global village. In some cultures, like that of the

Kalahari Bushmen, a person's story is considered his greatest treasure, his most sacred resource. Without stories, how would we live? We develop personal and cultural mythologies to help us lead our lives, the most significant Western cultural myth of the past two thousand years being the story of a truly special historical figure: Jesus.

That is, until the mid-nineteenth century, when the modern era jump-starts itself to life with Nietzsche's annunciation of the Death of God. Nietzsche's proclamation marked the end of the Jesus metamyth and the beginning of the search for a new story which would help us structure and lead our lives. But, no matter what metamyth we subscribe to, we realize that classical story structure is not arbitrary; it mimics life and nature:

Act I—Birth, spring, innocence, vitality;
Act II—Summer and fall, maturation and
    disillusionment;
Act III—Winter, death, despair.
And sometimes, there is an epilogue or
Act IV—a new spring, rebirth, resurrection.

Viktor Frankl, in his seminal post-Holocaust work, *Man's Search for Meaning*, demonstrated convincingly that man cannot survive without a reason for living, a personal narrative that provides him with *meaning*. Ironically, it was Freud, the atheist, who inadvertently brought God back to life. You see, in studying the psyche of the individual, Freud provides us with a solution to finding meaningful stories in our cynical, nihilistic age. Freud proposed that "the path to health involves the de-repression of hidden memories and the reconstruction of the individual's personal history" (for more on this see Sam Keen, *To a Dancing God*). Thus, the crucial history that must be recovered is familial, not communal, and in this act of retrieval, the human drama, played out as a specific story, transcends the individual to speak to society as a whole. In other words, in the story of one person is the story of all people, and so when you tell your story, you are telling the story of humanity, endowing life with meaning and a sense of the divine. Storytelling is a part of us, programmed deep within our DNA. Look at the ancient cave paintings in Lascaux, France. They are not static portraits but moving images, the first movies, the first recorded signs of man's need to tell stories, to empower himself and perpetuate the race. His survival hinged upon it. Simply put, if caveguy number one could convey to caveguy number two how he slayed the animal that was his primary source of nourishment, he could hoist his children up onto his shoulders instead of forcing them to stand on the ground and start from the same place he did decades earlier. Stories give us a proverbial "leg up" and represent the building blocks of society. Progress, forward motion, human betterment—they are all cultural myths, stories we tell ourselves.

In keeping with this discussion, let me illustrate this point by telling you another story.

Once upon a time, many, many years ago, everybody believed that the Sun revolved around Earth. You need only look up at the heavens to see how easily one could be convinced of the truthfulness of this story.

This story lasted for thousands of years and was well told by Ptolemy and others before him. Then, in the 1500s, Nicky Copernicus appears and says, "Whoa, hey kids, let's reevaluate this. Call me crazy, but I've got a hunch that maybe Earth revolves around the Sun and we can't tell because we're moving along with it. Maybe, just maybe, you and I aren't the center of the universe after all!"

Then, seventy years later or so, Galileo peers through his homemade telescope and collects even more proof of Copernicus' theory. Unfortunately, as a result, Galileo was labeled a heretic, put on trial by the Spanish Inquisition, and imprisoned. In order to save his hide, Galileo had to recant his findings and do all the things that writers have to do for producers and studio executives if they want to stay on the project. But on a more positive note, many years after Galileo died, poor, humiliated, and blind, the church changed its mind, enshrined him for his courage and admitted that maybe, just maybe, Earth does move . . . a little.

Stories are essential, but they are also always in flux; they need to be readjusted, tweaked, and, once in a while, new and original tales need to be created to ease our way through transitional moments.

: The Golden Rule of Change

But what exactly is the best storytelling form? Well, Aristotelian structure seems to have worked for thousands of years, so let's start there.

In his *Poetics*, Aristotle talked about how all stories must have a beginning, a middle, and an end (three acts) in which a protagonist journeys through "a series of experiences which leads to a climactic moment toward the end where he learns something, discovers something about himself that he could have known all along, but was blind to. This discovery comes as such an emotionally shattering blow that it changes the entire course of his life— *and that change must be for the better*" (this is Josh Logan's "golden rule" and can be found in his autobiography).

Note the emphasis on change and betterment. Nobody wants to pay eight dollars for a movie ticket or sixty or seventy-five dollars for a theater ticket to see something that they can see on the street for free.

Thus, when we include the word betterment in the mix, we see that writing is a highly moral act. True, there are cases where betterment comes too late, or never comes (unconventional tragedies like *Midnight Cowboy*, *Thelma & Louise*, and even, *The Godfather II*, which features the unforgettable final image of Michael Corleone sitting alone in his glass office while the sound of his brother being shot echoes through his mind, forever). Yet even these tragedies are, at their cores, highly moral. And most story product in post-Reagan-era Hollywood is not tragedy but hero myths, what the Greeks would call comedies: stories which are driven by our need for eternal redemption and happy endings.

For example, in *On Moral Fiction*, John C. Gardner states, "True art clarifies life, establishes models of human action, casts nets toward the future, carefully judges our right and wrong directions, celebrates, and mourns. It does not rant. It does not sneer or giggle in the face of death, it invents prayers and weapons. It designs visions worth trying to make fact. It does not whisper or cover or throw up its hands and bat its lashes. . . . It strikes lightning or *is* lightning."

So let your writing crackle with lightning, but never forget that a storm is one percent lightning and ninety-nine percent wind and rain. Yes, the reality of our lives is simply that we yearn for betterment because most people don't change. Your uncle is the same stubborn bastard that he was ten years ago and he will probably go to the grave that same stubborn bastard. Thus, I do not want to option the rights to your uncle's life. However, if your uncle's a stubborn bastard who learns, who changes; if he's the grand dragon of the Ku Klux Klan who falls in love with his Latina maid, learns she's infertile, then adopts forty Mexican orphans and ends up becoming a Cesar Chavez type, leading the movement for reform of the conditions of Latino migrant workers—that's a story I'll gladly part with eight bucks to see.

Think of it this way: We go to the theatre or the movie house to sit in a dark womb with a bunch of strangers and vicariously experience this human transformation. Like the Greeks, for whom theater was a communal and religious gathering wherein the fears and desires of the culture could be exorcised and expressed, modern day plays and movies let us come together to create a new sense of the community we have lost and in doing so, perpetuate a new set of metamyths which can provide answers to the hard questions of being alive. Humans want to grow, and we will pay to see the transformation of other human beings. By watching someone experience an epiphany and change, I too am transformed. All in two hours for a mere eight dollars, while most therapists charge at least a hundred an hour.

But, c'mon now dude, is it really necessary to have this change, this epiphany, by the end of the story?

Yes. *No character arc, no change, no movie. Try again, Kemosabe.* As for epiphanies, James Joyce defined them as "a sudden spiritual manifestation whether in the vulgarity of speech or of gesture or in a memorable phrase of the mind itself. It is for the artist to record these epiphanies with extreme care, seeing that they themselves are the most delicate and evanescent of moments." And so, it seems to me that they are the heart and soul of any worthwhile tale; they are inherently linked to good storytelling. Without them, just forget about it, pack up your things, turn your computer off and start again some other day.

And finally, if you need to reduce a story to its most fundamental elements, you would have to define them as follows:

A likable protagonist overcomes tremendous odds to reach a desirable goal, or something important happens to change someone we care about, or boy meets girl, girl gets boy in a pickle, boy gets pickle in girl, or we get our hero up into a tree, we throw rocks at her, and then we get her down safely.

For those who like such things, here are the essentials you need to tell a story that movie-going audiences will want to see:

1. Your main character must have a strong goal. Without being overly reductive, don't forget to ask yourself, "What does my main character want?" Establish specific character traits that distinguish this character from any other. This makes him or her memorable, quirky, and ripe for reversals. Make our hero a sympathetic character with whom we can connect. They don't have to be the nicest person in the world, only they must be inherently interesting. I wouldn't want Bobby De Niro in *Raging Bull* and Nicolas Cage in *Leaving Las Vegas* as my friends or relatives, and in fact, I don't really even like them, but heck, they are compelling, and I want, I care, I need to see what happens to them.

2. What or who is keeping our protagonist from achieving his or her goals? Remember, the goal must be an expression of an inner need. Which leads to . . .

3. Why do they want what they want? This is the stuff that is going on inside which drives them, and we must find a way to illustrate this externally.

4. And then, how in the end do they achieve or fail to achieve their goal, and why?

In a nutshell, you can think of a story as similar to the ancient art of alchemy, whose practitioners attempted to turn lead (Pb) into gold (Au). Start your story with an apparently stable status quo that is disturbed by a catalyst which sends things into a state of flux, transition, and disorder. As a result of this chaos, new ele-

The Alchemy of Screenwriting

ments are formed which allow for transformation, alchemy, change, leading to a new state of equilibrium which is similar to, yet different from, the original status quo. In other words, your story idea is turned from ordinary lead into a golden, polished script.

As I close this letter, the pivotal question reappears one final time, *Why write?* Do we write because of some primeval need to record, or for therapeutic catharsis? Is writing a form of deep personal analysis, or a facile attempt to capture a moment, a person, an event, on paper? Is it a yearning to leave something behind, something permanent, poetic, immortal? The answers are plentiful and diverse, but for many people, the answer is simply this: We write because we have to. And in the end, it seems the best answer.

That is all and it is more than enough.

Do not digest on an empty stomach and avoid reading while driving heavy machinery.

All the best,

Your Highly Esteemed Tutor

1/8/99

Dear Highly Esteemed Tutor:

Wow! Under that cranky, prehistoric veneer is a human being. Who would have thought? More, more, more! Can you be specific in terms of screenplay format? Pretty please, with Nutrasweet on top. Also, which books should I read as a supplement to my education?

Awaiting your next entry,

Bated Breath

P.S. I know you don't want to talk about your personal life, and I respect that; however, since I'm a highly visual person, I'd appreciate a recent photo of you. All I've ever seen is an old snapshot from *Who's Who*. It doesn't have to be professional, just some image of you that I can have when I imagine you lecturing to me.

2/2/99

Dear Bated Breath:

You should scrape your tongue to rid it of the foul-smelling bacteria that lead to your trenchmouth and breathing difficulties. With regard to my recent physical appearance, just think about what God might look like . . . there you have it . . . only with less facial hair, and younger.

Otherwise, you asked about format and books. Let's start there. Writers tend to be avid readers who believe that they can learn and master just about anything by reading about it. The truth is, reading *can* make a difference; yet, no matter how many books you read, the key to becoming a better writer lies in the disciplined and monotonous practice of putting one's buttocks into a seat and writing. However, since it is unhealthy to write all day long, there should be time allotted for family, loved ones (note, these may be different people), food, sleep, sex (hopefully?), movie-watching, and the reading of certain books that may prove to be inspiring and edifying.

The following short list represents a Whitman's Sampler of works of literature that you ought to be familiar with. There is a plethora of so-called writing handbooks, some better than others. Read as many as you can, gleaning a little from each. Among some of my personal favorites are Aristotle's *Poetics*, Michael Hauge's *Writing Screenplays That Sell*, Richard J. Walter's *Screenwriting*, Linda Seger's *Making a Good Script Great*, Anne Lamott's *Bird by Bird*, John Howard Lawson's *Theory and Technique of Playwriting* (almost impossible to find, but well worth any price), David Howard & Edward Mabley's *The Tools of Screenwriting*, and Rainer Maria Rilke's *Letters to a Young Poet*. Also valuable is the poetry of

Robert Frost, Pablo Neruda, Diane Wakoski, Philip Levine, and David St. John, as well as the fiction of T. Coraghessan Boyle, Charles Bukowski, John Cheever, John Updike (wherein you'll find the secrets to life), Kate Braverman, and anything by Annie Dillard. If your writing seems to be falling flat, go back to Faulkner; if your sense of the absurd seems to be on the wane, go to *Without Feathers* by Heywood Allen; to help you write concise, powerful, screenwriterly stage descriptions, go straight to Raymond Chandler. Plunge into Stephen Hawking's writings on the universe. Pore over Diane Ackerman's books, *A Natural History of the Senses* and *A Natural History of Love*. Study all the Nobel Prize for Literature acceptance speeches, especially William Faulkner's. Analyze C. G. Jung, Joseph Campbell, and all the Native American myths you can get your hands on. Peruse Harold Goddard's two books on the works of Shakespeare, and then go back and read Shakespeare again.

If you like to write with music playing in the background, listen to Aretha Franklin, Simon & Garfunkel, Sammy Davis Jr., Ella Fitzgerald, Jackson Browne, Rebbesoul, Van Morrison, Barbra Streisand, Cat Stevens, Enya, and anything by Stephen Sondheim; avoid Andrew Lloyd Webber and anything grungy or techno; cover the walls of the room you write in with paintings by Chagall, Klimt, and Gauguin; watch every movie starring Charlie Chaplin, Buster Keaton, Harold Lloyd, and Wallace & Gromit; study Ingmar Bergman, but not when you're depressed; avoid anything Quentin Tarantino has done since *Pulp Fiction*; focus instead on Preston Sturges, Alfred Hitchcock, and Stanley Kubrick. Watch movies on large screens, especially in multiplex theaters where you can sneak around and see two or three films in an evening; avoid getting caught; and most important, shun anything on videocassette unless it is either a movie you are unable to view on a big screen, or one you have to study scene by scene.

Go to your local public library. Don't read, just watch other people read.

Travel around the world and then come back home only to realize that everything you need is already there. Emily Dickinson never left her house. Chagall lived all over the world, but his canvases all emerged from his childhood and his childlike soul. Avoid writing in public places, especially coffee houses (way too faux artsy-fartsy), but if you have to write outside your home, write in airports, on planes, and especially in the lavatories of planes. When all else fails, get ahold of audio tapes (Marianne Williamson is good for inspiration, as is anything by Anthony Robbins, Robert Bly, Sam Keen, Zen prophet Alan Watts, and especially Clarissa Pinkola Estes). Play them in your suburban sport utility vehicle and surround yourself with language while you idle away the hours in traffic. But please, make sure you listen to the appropriate tape at the appropriate time. Raymond Carver's short stories are wonderfully dense, but if you are trying to bring your screenplay or stage play to life with luxurious language, Carver represents a poor choice.

After teaching screenwriting for many years, I have come to believe that there are many aspiring screenwriters around the globe who have what it takes, especially the psychological unease! So go forth: Even if you don't live in Tahiti, you can still be the Gauguin of your day. But always be careful—your soul is coated with Velcro, and as a result, you must scrape off most of what attaches to you before you become a post-it-pad person covered with thousands of tiny, multihued fluorescent squares, wandering the streets aimlessly, asking strangers, "Are you my mother?"

: **Format**

If you want to be a professional writer, your work should look as if it were written by a professional. This means using proper screenplay format. If you have the money to buy them, there are many software programs designed to help you format your work. If you don't have the money, you can use the tabs on your computer keyboard or typewriter. Either way, you need to know how your pages should look. As an example, I have reprinted the first page of an old screenplay of mine (see p. 50) which should serve as a suitable model. (Since it dealt with substantial historical, political, and cerebral issues, it was, of course, never made.)

Note that the font is Courier, 12-point. The margin needs to be larger (one-and-a-half inches) on the left side to accommodate the binding, which should be a single round-head brass fastener in each of the three holes. CUT TO's are rarely used anymore and formats do differ, but in general, there should be four comfortable margins (at least one inch wide) and most scripts average around fifty-two lines per page.

Also note that very few camera angles are specified. This is an example of the master scene format that has taken Hollywood by storm in these highly efficient, post-modern times. The main thing to understand here is that you are not the director. You are merely the writer, the architect, the drawer of the blueprint upon which the movie will be based. Yes, you're the creative genius, the mastermind behind it all and without you, nothing would be possible, but still, yours is not to choose which camera angle will be used in what situation. Give only as much information as you must to create a series of stunning images in the mind's eye of your reader.

In addition, the writing should be easy to read. Writing for the screen is different than writing for your English composition class; there is no need to impress with the literary quality of your prose.

FADE IN—

EXT. TROTSKY'S HOUSE/FORTRESS, MEXICO CITY—DAY

A concrete-walled fortress on Avenida Vienna in Coyoacan,
Mexico. A quaint Mexican street in which the only noise is
the sound of chirping birds.

ZOOM across crowded, noisy, dirty Mexican City streets until
we reach a high, strong concrete wall. The CAMERA floats above
the wall and dips down into a lush paradise—Trotsky's garden,
located in the heart of his fortress.

INT. TROTSKY'S FORTRESS—DAY

Inside the concrete walls is Trotsky's garden, filled with
trees, cactus, flowers, pre-Columbian Aztec sculptures and
singing birds. There is one large iron gate which connects the
outside world to this idyllic inner sanctum.

On the left is a hutch filled with rabbits. Exotic wire cages
filled with colorful chirping birds hang from the trees. Along
the far left wall is a black tripwire.

On the right is a door leading into a living/dining room. A
story above the living/dining room is Trotsky's study and
balcony, which looks out over the garden.

In the center of the garden a young Mexican girl, SILVIA, 16,
cradles the limp body of LEON TROTSKY, 60, who has bloody
white sheets wrapped around his wounded head. Trotsky's wife,
NATASHA SEDOVA, 60, watches on in horror.

Silvia takes Trotsky's hand and holds it against her chest.
Trotsky begins to shiver and his teeth chatter.

                    TROTSKY
        It's so cold . . .

Silvia holds him close to her chest, like a mother cradling
her newborn child.

                              MATCH DISSOLVE TO:

THE GARDEN—MANY YEARS LATER—

The CAMERA pulls back to reveal that Silvia is now in her
mid-thirties, and the years have not been kind to her.

                    SILVIA(V.O.)
        It is 1962. Late August. The time when the big
        breeze blows over the mountains . . .

In fact, overwriting is a major sin in screenwriting, and in many cases, full sentences aren't even necessary. Which leads us to the hirsute beast known as style. Essentially, a screenplay should be all action verbs and nouns, with very few adjectives and hardly any adverbs. The only information that appears should be that which facilitates the reader's visualization of your story concept. Everything else should be edited out. However, if you read many of the screenplays that are sold today, you'll see cutesy asides that are made specifically to the reader and information which could never make it onto the screen (like smells or inner psychological stuff). This is a stylistic choice and if you believe it will add pleasure to the reading experience, throw it in, but be advised: Screenwriting is not a literary form. You don't have to be Saul Bellow, and no one will care about your use of metaphors. In the end, screenwriting simply comes down to this:

THE WRITER'S & READER'S CONTRACT OF TRUTH

Writer: I am going to tell you the truth.

Reader: I am going to believe you, I am going to suspend my disbelief, but I am only one false line of dialogue or unmotivated action away from reestablishing my disbelief. I can't help myself from always thinking, could this really happen? Does this story satisfy me intellectually, emotionally, viscerally? Does it move me? Touch me? Where? How? Remember above all, *film is a visual and visceral medium,* not a verbal or cerebral one. Don't tell me, show me with riveting images. As Bishop Berkeley said, "To be is to be perceived." So show your audience (don't tell them) what they need to know, and they will follow you anywhere.

Still, there are times when the story seems to fail, when something about it does not ring true. This pulls me out of the story, snaps me out of my trance and forces me to think, "Hey! Wait a second. C'mon now, this couldn't happen!" When this occurs, the writer has failed to obey the rules of the world that were originally established. For example, if there are aliens in your movie, fine, but you must hint of their existence early; you can't just have aliens show up in the last ten minutes out of nowhere to save the day. In other words, *Aliens ex machina* is a big no-no and in fact, illegal in the state of Georgia. Crucial elements must be planted early and brought to fruition later.

: The Evelyn Krevolin Rule of Screenwriting

The penalty for not sowing and cultivating the seeds of believability early and often first became clear to me when I used to watch movies with my mother, Evelyn Krevolin (yes, that's her real name). Whenever we'd be sitting in a movie theatre or at home in front of the television, and a hole in the story appeared, she would always poke me in the ribs and say, "C'mon! That would never happen. That's stupid!"

And you know what? She was always right. Even though she wasn't a writer, she intuitively sensed a problem in the story. You see, when the writer's hand becomes visible in its efforts to cover gaping holes, and as a result we see action or hear dialogue which does not fit into the story's scheme or is inconsistent with the characters as established, we are disturbed, and rightfully so. Action must flow and not just occur to further the plot. In other words, *if it ain't organic, it ain't allowed.* Like the all-powerful hand of the cartoonist which starts to erase Daffy Duck when he begins to get a mind of his own, you must control your characters instead of letting them control you.

And so we bear witness to the rise of one of the basic tenets of storytelling, the Evelyn Krevolin Rule of Screenwriting, in which the parameters of the world can include anything, but once they are established, they may not be broken, or else your audience will feel like they're getting a good poke in the ribs. And we all know how much audiences want to be stroked, not poked!

A good story should grab the reader immediately and keep him or her turning the page. Every development person in Hollywood has stacks of screenplays to get through and is dying to find a reason not to finish yours. Don't give them one.

: **The Blessing and Curse of the American Writer**

I hope I am not coming across as, God forbid, anti-Hollywood, and as a result, anti-American. Nothing could be further from the truth. I believe that as a neophyte American writer, you have an arduous journey ahead. Yet, your lack of literary notoriety and success can be reframed into a blessing, especially if seen in terms of the American experience.

You see, other writers, those born in many other countries and cultures, come into this world with a wellspring of mythologies to be influenced, crushed, and stultified by. However, due to the fact that you are from the good old U.S. of A., a nation founded upon a massive genocidal campaign against the native inhabitants, you have the chance to emerge straight out of the earth, cleansed of ideology, like Athena's emanation from Zeus' head; you have the rare opportunity to burst forth into a land with no past, no collective unconscious, no stagnating pool of memory, of unifying myths, legends, and fables which dictate all your actions and tenets of morality. You have the chance to create the myths and legends that will guide this fair land through the millennium and into the twenty-first century.

This then, is the blessing and the curse of the American writer: the obligation and the freedom to create one's own mythology.

Take it seriously; it is no easy task. Be justifiably intimidated by its burden, and then rise to the occasion by telling great stories, vital metamyths that elevate men and women rather than downsize them; that speak of the greatness of humanity, not of its pettiness; that talk of the potential of human nature for redemption and transformation, not shallowness and stagnation; that urge us to strive to greater heights instead of the lowest common denominator. Have your characters lead us to the knowledge that we are no longer destined to repeat the mistakes of the past. Give us characters that beg us to constantly reinvent ourselves in new lights, cleaner, clearer, purer halogen bulbs that illuminate the good way, the just and right way.

So now, as you search for a place to enter the untamed forest, don't settle for a well-trodden path. Don't settle down, don't settle in, don't settle. Someone has to blaze trails, hold up a vanilla scented candle for the huddled masses. Someone is destined to be the voice of the twenty-first century; why not you? Write as if your voice can and will make a difference and what you might find is that one day, just maybe, you *will* be hailed as the voice of the next era.

To become this voice, don't hoard your best material. Squander it. Now. Put your best foot forward. It is harder to break in than it is to stay in. Use all your best lines and scenes now. Don't worry. When you are ready to write your next piece, you will have accumulated more material. And by that time, you will probably be obsessed by many other important new themes. Sure, even the best writers run into roadblocks and need breaks to recharge their batteries, but if you just keep working, you will never dry up like a riverbed during a drought. Keep working and the words will keep coming. Trust me on this one. Keep writing; the act of writing itself is the key. It should become the central focus, safe haven, and metaphor of your life. Remember, the difference between writers and people who write is the difference between bullfighters and bullshitters.

So, let your voice reverberate in the dark night and never, I repeat, never remain silent. That is the cardinal sin of the writer. Speak, let your voice ring true and listen for the echo, the ramifications of your words. And if you are truly speaking from your marrow, you will see that your language resonates in the bones of all mankind. Write, let your words sing, and then sit back, cross your fingers, and pray. You can do nothing more and there is nothing else that is more valuable to your own growth as well as that of all people. I repeat: Write, let your words sing, and then sit back, cross your fingers, and pray.

And have fun with it.

That is all.

And May God Bless You,

The Cardinal

Writing Exercise #1:

Please write three scenes:

1. In the first scene, your main character arrives to meet someone and the environment feels strange, mysterious, awkward.

2. In the second scene, your main character reenters this same environment (it could be the next day or ten years later). He or she is greeted by the same person from the first scene, but this time, the environment and the greeting feel warm, happy, positive.

3. In the third scene, as your main character reenters this same environment, the person they are hoping to see is not there. The environment reflects a feeling of desolation, sadness, and alienation.

Don't use dialogue. Instead, use visual imagery and action (the basis of the filmic lexicon) to dictate mood and story. And yes, I want you to create a compelling narrative, most of which takes place offstage and must be deduced from what is given in the three distinct, disparate scenes. Good luck, and don't make easy choices—make daring ones.

4. Also write a one-page character biography of the protagonist which includes aspects of backstory, physical characteristics, and personality traits. Once this is written, see how many of these aspects you can incorporate into the story in subtle and artful ways.

3/11/99

Dear Cardinal:

On the following page, please find writing exercise numero uno. I hope you get a kick out of it. Feel free to trash it accordingly. In addition, can you be more specific about the significant story turning points and ensuing page numbers that I should be conscious of when I'm writing a script that corresponds to Hollywood standards?

I remain your ever faithful and humble servant,

Hard at Work in Washington

P.S. Okay, I know we made a pact not to discuss your personal life, but how about mine? Don't you want to get to know me better?

Writing Exercise #1: Dr. Grader

```
A. FADE IN:

INT. LABORATORY—NIGHT

The room stands dark, silent . . .

Suddenly, the symmetrical rows of
fluorescent lights flash to life like stale
lightning.

Each flicker gives a brief glimpse of the
laboratory. The walls are a bright white,
clean, unused. At every few intervals stand
```

stainless steel plating, signifying the entrance to a walk-in freezer or cabinet holding a myriad of medical supplies and scientific instruments.

A counter top which encircles the entire room is forged of the same cold steel. Rows of beakers and graduated cylinders line the walls like glass soldiers.

The flickering stops, as dull fluorescent light fills the room in an anesthetized bath, highlighting a large table in the middle of the laboratory.

Roughly three feet off the floor, held by a huge steel column at its center, the slick metal table resembles an autopsy counter, only at each end are placed several steel shackles. The room is cold, sterile, and empty.

A MAN, early 30s, stands at the door. Wire-rimmed glasses encircle his dark eyes which dart around the room. The black frames of his glasses serve as a stark contrast to his red hair, the color of cooling molten rock, which highlights his granite features.

His young eyes slowly pan the room until they focus on the center table.

Walking forward, he runs his finely manicured hand across the cold gray surface. He presses down lightly, as if testing its strength.

Kneeling, he presses the side of his face against the steel, looking across the smooth surface.

Rising to his feet, he walks and sits down at a nearby steel alloy desk. The desk stands bare, except for a note which reads "Welcome Dr. Grader. Good luck."

The doctor now sits silently at the desk. He simply stares. We sense his troubling thoughts.

Finally, he stands again, and slowly makes his way to a huge metal door at the rear of the room. A complicated series of locks and latches line the perimeter of the massive door; they all click open in unison as he presses a sequence of numbers on a digital keypad.

The door opens, allowing a sea of liquid nitrogen vapor to escape onto the floor, encircling the doctor's face and body in a ghostly mist.

Cool green lights within the massive freezer paint a lime shimmer across his glass lenses.

INSIDE OF THE FREEZER—

We see a large glass cylinder, roughly two feet in diameter and four feet tall. Liquid nitrogen bubbles and percolates inside the glass, cooling the brain and spinal cord which reside within.

Dr. Grader offers a cunning smile as the lights flicker and MUSIC RISES . . .

FADE TO BLACK.

B. FADE IN:

INT. LABORATORY—NIGHT—MANY YEARS LATER

The laboratory stands in disarray. Various diagrams and mathematical equations hang from every wall, covering the cold steel in a collage of ink and paper.

Plastic champagne glasses and an assortment of bottles are scattered throughout the room, as are paper hats, streamers, and other signs of celebration.

The door opens, and the fluorescent lights instantly spring to life as Dr. Grader stumbles in, an empty bottle of Jack Daniels clutched in his paw.

His brilliant red hair has dulled to a crimson rust, with streaks of gray. His eyes, though tired and old, move like a child's at Christmas as he staggers across the room toward his desk.

Dr. Grader brushes an assortment of trash from his chair and collapses into it, the liquor acting as though it added fifty pounds to his weight.

Opening one of the many drawers, the doctor removes a stack of texts and notebooks, tossing them around the cluttered room as if he has no more use for them.

CLOSE UP—At the bottom of the drawer lies the faded WELCOME note, now grown sickly yellow.

Dr. Grader holds the note up to his face attempting to focus his drunken eyes upon the words. He finally recognizes it, and laughs hysterically.

Taking the note in one hand, he crumples it into a small ball, throws it amidst the other debris around the room and takes another swig from his bottle.

Smiling, he attempts to stand up again, fails, and finally manages to stagger over to the main table.

ON THE STEEL TABLE—

Is the striking figure of a young MAN. He is over six feet tall, his pale skin pulled taut over a muscular frame. Long needles protrude from his arms and legs, leading back up into a complex series of chemicals and electrodes above the table. The red hair and features of the man slightly resemble the doctor, though certain parts have been . . . exaggerated.

With a gleeful, childlike giggle, Dr. Grader kneels next to his creation, brushing his fingers through the man's red hair. He looks upon the silent figure as he would upon his son.

In the freezer in the background, the glass cylinder stands empty . . .

FADE TO BLACK.

C. FADE IN:

INT. LABORATORY—DAY—A FEW WEEKS LATER

The scattered bottles and spilt champagne have now been replaced with blood. The once uniform fluorescent lights dangle from their sockets, swinging silently like glowing pendulums.

The doctor, a massive, still fresh scar across the right side of his face, partially hidden beneath an eye patch, wearily walks across the room.

An occasional silent explosion of sparks showers the laboratory, highlighting the dented steel doors and frayed, exposed electrical wiring.

Slowly, and with a somber mask, the doctor walks to the center table. His hands run over the steel shackles, now reduced to twisted scrap metal.

A small puddle of dried blood paints a sickening picture across the steel platform, as the doctor runs his hand over his scar, remembering the massacre.

Taking his glasses off, placing them on his overturned desk, the doctor walks to a far corner of the room.

On the distant counter lay two severed arms; at their stumps extend a massive series of digital wires and titanium skeleton. The hands are covered in the dull crimson of dried blood, as a row of black bullet holes line the forearms and biceps.

Unable to bear looking at the severed limbs, Grader grabs them and throws them across the floor, causing another flash of sparks to fall to the ground.

Making his way around the hanging fluorescent lights and scattered debris, the doctor approaches the large freezer.

The door is now dented, the locks hang broken and worthless, as a flow of liquid nitrogen mist streams freely from the cracked steel.

Yielding to creaking hinges and the dull roar of steel against steel, Grader opens the door to reveal the glass cylinder.

INSIDE THE FREEZER—

The doctor stares at the contents of the glass cylinder: the same brain and spinal cord as before. Only now, a section of the right hemisphere of the brain is missing, the serrated edges scarred with black powder burns and riddled with bullets.

The sad eyes of the doctor look at the motionless organ. Grader inhales and then exhales loudly.

BACK TO THE LAB—

Closing the door, the doctor turns around and begins the long walk to the exit.

In the dark cylinder, the spinal cord twitches with a small spasm, its base brushing up against the glass.

Hearing the slight noise, the doctor stops, and turns around. Dr. Grader scurries back towards the freezer, lifts up the cylinder, embraces it passionately and holds his dying child in his arms . . .

FADE TO WHITE.

THE END?

CHARACTER BIO OF DR. ALEXANDER GRADER

Raised during the height of the "free love" movement in the late 1960s, Dr. Alexander Grader had always believed in serving the public good. However, Dr. Grader's view of the public good often differed vastly from popular consensus. A genius medical student at the University of California, Berkeley, Dr. Grader failed to graduate when he was expelled for punching the head professor in the face following an argument about genetic manipulation. Unable to obtain a job at any hospital due to this incident, Dr. Grader plunged into depression and despair, while his skills died away in a flood of cheap alcohol.

At the bottom of his life, and only a few years out of medical school, Dr. Grader met the chairman of a high-tech commercial research company in the Bay Area through a bizarre accident. Saving the chairman's life from a runaway trolley, Dr. Grader was offered a debt of thanks and a warm meal. However, the chairman soon realized that his life wasn't saved by some bum, but by a medical and scientific genius. Immediately offering his savior a job, the chairman gave Dr. Grader a position in the company doing genetic and cloning research, and experiments dedicated to preserving and prolonging human life.

Though raised in a moral family and taught the virtues of freedom and love in college, Dr. Grader has always been a highly competitive and steadfast man. Once setting his mind on a goal, Dr. Grader never strays from it or allows anything to get in his way. Though this is an admirable quality, it is also a personal shortcoming, as Dr. Grader never has had the time to find a wife or raise a family. The fleeting relationships he did have revolved around purely sexual needs, as he was always dedicated to his first and only love—hard science.

A powerful man, resembling someone who would be more at home in the Alaskan tundra than in a research lab, Dr. Grader often uses his obvious strength to "influence" the opinions of co-workers who might not agree with his point of view . . .

5/6/99

Dear Hard:

I'm sure you've lived a truly scintillating life, which you find eternally captivating, but, to be blunt, I don't care to get to know you through anything other than your work. So, let's get to it. Ah, so much better than *Convertible Man.* I'm glad to see it. Keep writing. Now on to our next lesson.

The single most important concept that I want to convey to you during this, our second big lesson, is what I have come to call "concretizing the abstract." This is a term which I believe I am the first to utilize, especially considering the fact that I coined it.

So then, what exactly does "concretizing the abstract" mean? Well, for me to answer that question, let us start at the beginning. Since film is a visual medium, the screenwriter does not have the luxury of the novelist, who can convey psychological states through interior monologues, detailed thoughts, and omniscient narrators. The only film technique that comes close to these novelistic devices is the voice-over, which tends to be overused, can be distracting to the viewer, and many times, is utilized in a lame attempt to compensate for a poorly told story. As in, let's try to save *Blade Runner* by forcing Harrison Ford to do some voice-overs. Sure, it makes the film a little less murky, but in the end, it's more annoying than helpful.

Yes, there are times when voice-overs add to the filmic texture, but these are few and far between. In general, you should avoid them and develop your visual storytelling skills; in other words, you should learn to *concretize the abstract*, to physically embody your characters' abstract emotional states of mind in concrete manifestations such as symbolic props, actions, and objects.

You see, by merely listening to the dialogue uttered by the thespians on the silver screen, we can't know what's really going on inside the characters' minds, especially if they aren't talented performers. Therefore, it's your obligation as the writer to externally convey the complex interior states of your characters. It is your number one priority as someone who writes for moving pictures to *concretize the abstract.* To externalize emotions. With this in mind, you will be able to avoid relying on weak, on-the-nose dialogue which lamely presents emotional states, such as, "Wow! Today I'm so depressed!" or "Whoa boy, I feel so happy!" Try to use what T. S. Eliot termed an *objective correlative*—an object that correlates to emotional states of the characters.

So then, when we are writing for the screen, we want to think of scenes in terms of images, not words. Don't rely on dialogue for exposition, let the images provide the exposition. And please, always remember the cardinal rule of writing workshops across this fair land: *Show me don't tell me!*

You want your audience to enter what Joseph Campbell called a state of aesthetic arrest—a temporary state of being in which one loses all sense of time and place and becomes lost in the world of the text; where there is no distinction between the proscenium and the chairs in the balcony, the screen and the seats, the actors and the audience, I and thou; there is only the shared moment of wonder. The audience surrenders all rational thought and allows the power of the moment to overwhelm them, to transport them from their aching joints, complaining spouses, financial problems, and drop them into the magical world of the story. Think of it as a reverse of *The Purple Rose of Cairo*, where instead of the main character stepping out into the audience, each member of the audience steps into the main character's role on the screen.

Let me provide you with an example of this phenomenon. You are sitting in the movie theatre watching *The Lost World*. It's the scene where the mean old raptors chase the good guys into the abandoned warehouse. Just as the good guys are about to get eaten by the raptors, your ever-playful significant other sitting next to you forms his or her hand into a claw, shrieks, and scrapes the side of your neck. Your reflexes kick in and you do the only sane thing: you scream like a banshee, toss all your popcorn and jujubes into the air, pelting your neighbors and then, red-faced with humiliation and fear, you spend the rest of the film hiding under your seat.

So, now that you have a clear sense of what your priorities should be when you start writing, the next question that comes to mind should be, how do I start? Where do I start? HELP!!!

1. Well, a good place to begin might be this: Imagine what the one-sheet (the poster) might look like for your film. What one image would go on the poster? What headline might be written across the ad for your picture in the Sunday paper? Just one line. That is all . . . for now.

Don't be afraid to be reductive. Yes, we live in a highly complex world, but the minds of most Americans, especially those who work in the entertainment industry, are amazingly Rain Man-like. So, force yourself to have clarity. Simplicity is a virtue. Master the ten-second story pitch. What is the concept or premise of your film? What's the hook? Can you sell it in one line? For example, the way you would describe Steven Seagal's *Under Siege* is, simply, *Die Hard* on an aircraft carrier.

This emphasis on simplicity will ensure that your picture is a so-called high-concept (usually big-budget, star-driven, premise-oriented) movie, which many in the industry believe is the most commercially viable kind. Maybe the simplest way to define high-concept is to explain what it's not. Think of high-concept pieces as not the more artistic, theatrical, so-called soft, low-concept, character-driven pieces that, even though they may be very well written, are not as easily sold. And even if they are sold, the reason for the sale usually lies not in the script's concept, but the execution.

2. What is the reason you want—you need—to write this story? In one or two lines, give the theme (this work is thematically about how love conquers all, crime doesn't pay, etc.)

3. Now, write your story in a three- or four-line paragraph.

4. In three paragraphs (representing the three acts—beginning, middle, and end) tell the whole story.

That is enough . . . for now.

And once you start writing your pages, don't show off, don't use curlicues when you can use straight lines. Readers know very quickly when they are in the hands of a master, a person comfortable in his or her own writing self, so the writer doesn't come off as insecure and controlling, but instead, comes off as if they are *in control!*

Yes, control. This is a key word, and it is ultimately hinged upon another key word: trust. Trust the power of your writing to subtly convey all the necessary information to your audience; trust your words and if the reader doesn't get everything, that's okay, they might still get it on an unconscious level or even if they don't get it on that level, that's okay, maybe they'll get it next time around, and if they still don't get it, maybe it's time for a new reader who hasn't been lobotomized, or maybe, just maybe, it's your fault. Yes, I'm sorry to say it, but there is always the possibility that you can be too subtle. There is always the chance that you may have written something which is imperfect and you need to do another revision. Sorry folks, but writing is rewriting, although that's another lesson entirely.

Simply put, in every scene, every beat, every moment, know what you want your characters to do, and why. When a friend of mine was pitching his story to Steven Spielberg, the Amblin Man kept asking him, "What does the audience feel right now in this moment?" What do they feel? Know what you want your audience to feel all the time and then, manipulate those feelings to achieve your storytelling goals. However, don't forget the Evelyn Krevolin Rule of Screenwriting: Never tip your hand, never let the audience see what you are trying to do, for if they feel as if they are being lectured to or manipulated, they will instantly reject whatever is being said, no matter how valid it might be.

Since film is a visceral medium, if you appeal to your audience intellectually, you won't really have them until you've hooked them in the gut or grabbed them by the heart.

In the end, your work must stand on its own. Although it might be nice to attend every screening of your work, standing next to the screen with a long pointer, explaining all the symbolic imagery, you must trust that your work speaks for itself (especially if your movie appears on thousands of screens nationwide).

This issue of trust is a huge one for many writers, especially those who are aspiring. I know that most writers in film school either tend to overwrite their screenplays because they don't trust their readers, or they underwrite, planting their screenplays with so many obscure elements that there is no way in hell a reader will be able to pick up on any of them. In terms of my personal experiences, it was not until after I graduated from film school and started writing plays for the theater that I understood this concept of trust. It was only after working hand-in-hand with actors and directors, day in and day out, polishing, revising, and listening to my work being performed in front of live people that I finally started to intuitively sense audience needs and began to trust that my writing could fulfill them in a simple, straightforward manner.

As film is an invisible medium (the edits should be seamless to give the appearance of a flowing vision), so should your writing be seemingly organic, natural, without artifice. Audiences should believe that the actors are literally making it up as they go along. The dramatic arts are highly artificial, but done in such a way that they give the illusion of being without artifice.

Enough information for one letter, lest your mind overheat and explode.

Zey gezunt (Go in good health), kiddo,

Art

Writing Exercise #2:

Your second assignment is to find an objective correlative in modern stage drama and recent films. Then, explain how the author concretizes the abstract.

5/17/99

Dear Art:

I'm sad that you don't want to know more about me personally, but for now I will respect your wishes and allow you to get to know me exclusively through my work. Although I must say, I hope that one day we can talk about more than writing.

Now, my answer is: Tennessee Williams, *The Glass Menagerie.* Objective correlative: the glass unicorn whose horn gets broken in the second act by the gentleman caller. Yes, a fragile sensitive little glass unicorn figurine. Fanciful? Beautiful? Tragic? Poignant? Phallic? Call it what you will, but baby, it brings with it a host of emotions. When it happens on stage, frankly, it's damn powerful. (And I thought you should know, I was the stage manager in our community theater production.)

Or in modern films. One of my favorite objective correlatives has to be Clint Eastwood's—or should I say, Dirty Harry's—.44-caliber Magnum revolver. As soon as you see or hear about this gun, you think of Dirty Harry and it concretizes his abstract qualities of power, antiauthoritarianism, and danger.

Pretty good, huh? I bet you don't find students like me every day, now do you?

Your single favorite student of all time,

Dying for more

P.S. Oh My God! Your lessons rock and roll! Don't ever stop, especially with the easy homework assignments. Do I have an A so far, or what?

6/13/99

Dear Cocky One:

I think it's closer to an A-minus and slipping into the B range even as we speak. And be careful, you're going to strain your arm and bruise your back if you keep patting yourself so forcefully. So, my friend, don't turn into a prima donna on me now, especially considering how far we still have to go.

: Structure, Plot, and Theme

The three most important concepts that I want to convey to you next are structure, plot, and theme. As big Al Hitchcock once said, "Drama is life with the boring bits cut out." So, crack open the shells, toss 'em out, and then, munch away at the sweet pistachio meat inside, but be careful not to get red dye all over your fingers. Or, for the metaphorically impaired, a diamond is beautiful only when it is cut and polished correctly. So now, let us find out how to organize the chaos of life into something meaningful, something that is cast so precisely that when it is struck, it rings of poetic, artistic truth.

Film and theater are reality, only better; they are heightened, hyperreal. Life zips by like a VCR on super fast forward, but once in a while, there are moments that move in slow motion and remain stuck in our memories forever. They are there for a purpose. They have an inherent power. Explore these moments. Why are they unforgettable? Pick the most dramatic events of your life and start there, but don't be afraid to twist them around, to bend and shape them into art, so that they are always fresh and full of surprises.

Start with reality and then go from there toward art.

Now, as I mentioned earlier, you need to have a clear understanding of what story it is you are trying to tell. To help you do this, you should be able to articulate the answer to these two questions:

1. What is your story about?
2. What is your story about?

I know, I know, at first glance, these two questions appear to be similar, but in fact, they are worlds apart. The first question is one of plot. What is the A plot line? What is the dramatic problem or device that drives the film forward?

Now, the second question, which looks deceptively like the first, is simply, "What's your story about, you know, thematically?" What are you trying to say? The theme equals those elements in the film that are going to alter the way the audience thinks of the world after they leave the theater. This is where you are invited to be a little bit preachy, to have a point of view, to attempt to say something that can and should change the world. But if your theme is too obviously stated, if it crosses the boundaries of what audiences feel is acceptable, or if it presumes to take the place of a plot, you're in trouble. You see, the theme is the sinew holding together the bones of the story, it must exist as a subtext, as the roots to the story's blossom. The theme resonates throughout the story. For example, the film *Back to the Future* deals with the theme of sons inheriting the sins of their fathers. In this movie, Michael J. Fox sees his father being browbeaten by his father's arch-nemesis Biff, and Fox thinks of himself as worthless as well. But when Fox goes back to the past, he tells his father, "You can achieve anything you put your mind to." When he returns to the present, he sees that he has succeeded in changing his father and in doing so, lifted his family out of its cycle of failure.

As I stated earlier, all well-crafted stories hinge upon at least one major dramatic question which is established when the inciting incident takes place. Will Harry and Sally ever be able to get together as more than friends? The film's theme is inherent in this question. As the stakes change, as the characters face more jeopardy, as they make bigger and bigger choices, a story unfolds and in the end, if we look closely, we can see that this wonderful story was really a huge lie told to illustrate a simple truth: Love can triumph over all.

: **The Broomstick Engine**

All stories need a plot device that drives the story forward, what I like to call a "broomstick engine." This phrase is based upon L. Frank Baum's beloved classic *The Wizard of Oz*, in which the Wizard sends Dorothy, the Cowardly Lion, the Scarecrow, and the Tin Man on a mission. If they want the Wizard to grant them their wishes (respectively, home, courage, a brain, and a heart), they must bring him the broomstick of the Wicked Witch of the West. Thus, the broomstick serves as an engine, a powerful motivating device, what Hitchcock would call a "MacGuffin" driving the story forward. (Think of Rosebud in *Citizen Kane*.) The magnificence of *The Wizard of Oz* is that in their efforts to capture the broomstick, Dorothy and her friends inadvertently develop the attributes they were searching for all along. In essence, once they've achieved their immediate goal—the broomstick—they've also achieved their long-term goals (a way home, courage, a brain, and a heart), which are then validated by the Wizard's speeches and his presentation of tokens to each of them.

To further illustrate this important point, let me give you a specific example of an experience I had with a student within the hallowed halls of USC Film School. Student X (out of a sign of respect for the Hollywood Ten, I've never been one to name names) approached me with a story he'd been toying with for a long time but still wasn't happy with. The story told the tale of two college students who had to deal with the unexpected death of a close friend. Student X was a bright kid who wanted to say a lot about the nature of young people reconciling themselves with death. So he had a strong B storyline, but essentially no A storyline. He needed a broomstick engine to drive the thematic elements forward. The more we talked, the more I realized he needed a funeral somewhere far away to serve as his broomstick. He also lacked a strong antagonist, plot points, and complications to make the journey to the funeral work as a mirror reflecting the inner journey the main character had to undergo as he learned to reconcile himself with the inevitability of death.

In the end, the student's lesson was simply this: If you want to say something important, God bless you, but the world already has enough preachers. What the world needs now (besides love, sweet love) is more storytellers who thrill and entertain; and after you've been enthralled by the wondrous tale of the master yarn-spinner, you might find that good storytelling also includes subtle messages which are covertly hung on the clothesline of a compelling story.

: Beginnings and Endings

All plots tend to move deathward. This is the nature of plots. Political plots, terrorist plots, lover's plots, narrative plots . . .

—Don DeLillo, *White Noise*

The aim of all life is death.

—Sigmund Freud, *Beyond the Pleasure Principle*

The model proposes that we live in order to die, hence that the intentionality of the plot lies in its orientation toward the end even while the end must be achieved only through detour.

—Peter Brooks, *Reading for the Plot*

Movies evolved in the twentieth century as a commercial entertainment form in which formulaic dramas with conventional Aristotleian structure were mass manufactured to deliver audience rear ends into theater seats where they would be captive consumers of popcorn at exorbitant prices. The more popular the film, the more tickets sold; the more tickets sold, the more popcorn sold. And so, films that were popular with audiences = more popcorn = more $money$ made. Theater owners preferred popular films that tended to be different from but reassuringly similar to other popular films that audiences had already seen.

Hence, the rise of the Hollywood formulaic film with a story hinged upon a standard format in which a problem is introduced in the first act and solved by the third act which closes, inevitably, with a happy ending (or a tragic one with hopeful overtones). In the span of roughly 120 minutes, problems involving the protagonist (and in many cases, also a minor character in the B plot) are surmounted in order that the protagonist may learn a valuable lesson and be united with family, spouse, loved one, and insignificant others.

These happy endings, marked by the loving union of family members, represent an affirmation of the human need to surmount death through displays of love, acts of redemption, and attempts at transcendence in the form of familial continuance (represented in many cases by marriage and/or children) and collective memory. True, there has always been the classic American outlaw/anti-hero (think of Michael Corleone in *The Godfather* and

Humphrey Bogart as Rick in *Casablanca*) who represents a darker American apocalyptic vision, yet it is the Rambos, Ripleys, and Luke Skywalkers, the survivors who overcome death and tragedy, who are the truly immortal American heroes.

In order to discover more about the nature of beginnings and endings, I want to start by going back and exploring what is meant by traditional Aristotleian structure. In Gerald F. Else's 1967 translation of *Poetics*, Aristotle states that great drama is an imitation of an action which is complete and whole. More specifically:

> Whole is that which has beginning, middle and end. "Beginning" is that which does not necessarily follow on something else, but after it something else naturally is or happens; "end" the other way round, is that which naturally follows on something else, either necessarily or for the most part, but for nothing else after it . . .

Thus, average audience members, who are unconsciously attuned to this Aristotleian beginning, middle, and end model, will expect a certain structure *(energeia);* if they don't get it, they will feel vaguely unsatisfied. In the first act of the story, all the necessary elements must be assiduously planted, twisted and turned around in unexpected ways in the second act, and then paid off by the end of the third act. In other words, the ending serves as something

> . . . which naturally follows on something else, either necessarily or for the most part, but for nothing else after it . . . So, then, well-constructed plots should neither begin nor end at any chance point but follow the guidelines just laid down.

Another way to think of this theory of *energeiac* plots is summarized by John C. Gardner in his bible for modern writers, *The Art of Fiction*, which states that endings should embody the "actualization of the potential that exists in the plot and characters." And so, when we find out who Keyser Söze really is at the end of *The Usual Suspects*, we cheer. However, when a writer does not tie all his loose ends together, when he introduces elements that do not pay off, audience expectations are undermined. The predominating *energeiac* structures that viewers desire are turned on their collective head, audiences feel cheated, and in turn, can get pissed off and throw rotten tomatoes at you. For example, in the film *Con Air*, the writer realized that he needed to pay off the mother-daughter-bunny reunion with the main character (played by Nicolas Cage). After they have crashed landed in Las Vegas and gone on a ten-mile wild goose chase, the bunny just happens to drift by and the mother and daughter just happen to be standing in the near background for the big reunion scene. Of course, this scene is utterly implausible, and destroys any credibility that the film might once have had.

It is in comedic films where these brittle seams show the most. For example, in *Wayne's World*, the author realizes he must plant information about a satellite feed early in the story if Wayne is going to be able to achieve his goal in the climax. However, since it is so improbable that anyone would just happen to tell him all the information that he will need, when he does receive the info, Wayne turns to the camera and comments on how convenient it is that someone has told him all this. We laugh, and we also know that in the end when Wayne is able to subvert the bad guys and win the girl, Hollywood closure is achieved and audiences leave the theatre feeling happy, happy, happy.

My favorite example of a classic Hollywood beginning is the first shot in *Citizen Kane;* you remember, that famous sweeping camera pan which starts with a No Trespassing sign and continues inside Kane's mansion Xanadu until it reaches an extreme close-shot of Kane's mouth uttering the word "Rosebud," at which point the camera pulls back to reveal newsreel footage telling of Kane's life. Now, a little pop quiz to see if you're a real film buff.

Question: What is the last shot of *Citizen Kane?*

Answer: The last shot is the same as the opening one—a No Trespassing sign outside Xanadu.

Moreover, the initial image of the glass ball that is shattered is restored only at the very end of the film when the mystery of Rosebud is finally revealed. Yet, not wanting to oversimplify his film, Welles problematizes Rosebud by having a character say that this clue is not the entire solution to the *Citizen Kane* enigma, but "just a piece in a jigsaw puzzle, a missing piece."

In *Citizen Kane,* Welles practically invents a new form of story-telling in which he constructs his film as a topsy-turvy chronological jigsaw puzzle held together by flashbacks, beginning at the end with Kane's death and his final word—"Rosebud." In fact, Kane's utterance of "Rosebud" is a unifying filmic device, a focal point Welles thought he needed due to his fear that *Citizen Kane's* unconventional style might alienate the average viewer as well as the average studio executive. Indeed, Welles' instincts were correct; the Rosebud gimmick proved effective, and to this day, audiences still become engrossed with trying to discover what Rosebud really means.

: Structural Signposts

One more practical note: Yes my friend, there are certain basic page numbers which correspond to story points. Please remember, these are not God-given formulaic points set in stone, but only starting points, guideposts, foundation markers to help you navigate the almost overwhelming superstructure of an entire full-length feature. They are employed most vigorously by nonwriters, those members of the entertainment industry who "develop"(?!) the hard earned handiwork of writers. Lest we deny these hard-working D-people their due, these well-worn story points did not appear out of thin air. They are the result of many bright people watching many fabulous films over the course of many years and then tabulating approximate times in which audiences have come to expect certain plot events. In other words, whether you sub-scribe to Aristotle's theories or the plot points of screenwriting meta-guru Syd Field, both are reflecting assimilated expectations of audiences who have grown to expect a so-called classical story structure wherein the plot always turns after a certain period of time elapses. And in the end, if it ain't broke . . .

These formulas should provide support for the initial structuring of your story; however, there is always the possibility of them handcuffing you artistically. In order to avoid this problem, see these guidelines as a sort of flexible boundary, an invisible fence. If they seem to be hamstringing you, instead of throwing your hands up in despair, try to be like Picasso, who mastered the academic tenets of light, shadow, and perspective at a young age and then spent the rest of his life deconstructing these rules and learning how to see and paint like a child again. Yes, be childlike, not childish.

Remember, just because act breaks are not labeled or indicated doesn't mean that they aren't there. So for what it's worth, here we go:

ACT I— Lean cuisine turf/no fat allowed.
pp. 1–10: Set-up. Establish theme and tone; expose the heart of your picture. What is it about?

pp. 11–25: The story must be established. Your dramatic problem must be presented.

pp. 26–32: Turn your story in a new direction. Reversal. Discovery. Twist. POW! Leading us quickly to the end of ACT I: By page 32 your protagonist must experience a major turning point that sends us in another direction and changes the protagonist's life forever. This turning point must relate to the A story line. Also, the protagonist should confront the antagonist and now, the fun really begins.

ACT II— The longest act, and the most difficult one to write. This is also the only act where you can breathe, explore characters and relationships.

pp. 33–45: The B, C, and D (or subplot) storylines should have been established by now. These subplots deal with the main character's relationships, not the plot itself; for instance, the best friend, the parent, the love interest that affects the A storyline, but is not the driving force of the story.

Every ten minutes or every ten pages, I WANT ACTION—Boom-Boom-Boom. Never let up. Always keep building. Especially in action/adventure scripts. You always have to top yourself. In ensuing scenes, the audience believes there is no way the main character can get closer to death and still escape, but the writer always seems to find a plausible way out for the main character.

p. 60: The midpoint. Usually a high note that can only lead to a low note by the end of the second act. We can take a breather here, but we know it won't last for long.

p. 90: The second-act turning point—the major turning point for the protagonist, who should now be at his lowest possible moment . . . and THEN, has a realization

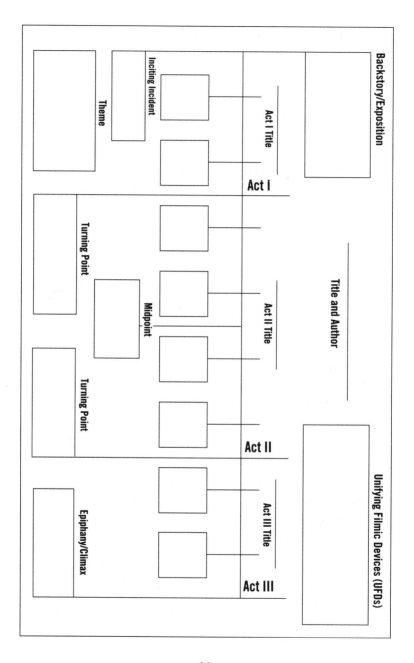

(the "Ah-Ha") which leads him to pick himself up by the bootstraps and rush headlong into the third act. This turning point affects the course of the rest of his or her life. It is a galvanizing moment—an essential plot point when the main character realizes something about herself or her world that she did not know before—and this epiphany changes her life forever. Our hero finds the courage to confront something she has never confronted before.

ACT III—A series of actions in which the loose ends are tied together, always building, rushing toward the climax and the end.

p. 110: Final jeopardy. Everything comes to a head. No more uncertainty. Usually a heightened experience.

p. 115: Epilogue. Now, get out fast.

p. 120: FADE OUT. THE END.

With these structural signposts in mind, you should be ready to utilize the scene-o-gram on p. 82, which is a variation on an original concept of a colleague, a wonderful screenwriting instructor at UCLA by the name of Hal Ackerman. This scene-o-gram is my own way of concretizing the abstract in terms of the major tenets of classic Hollywood story structure. It allows the writer to chart out the entire course of his story on one page . . .

: **Scene-O-Gram**

This scene-o-gram is a good starting point for you to see the major beats of your story. Fill in as much as you can, even things that will never appear in your movie, like the titles for each act. The more you can add to the scene-o-gram, the better sense you will get of your film (for example, see the *Mrs. Doubtfire* scene-o-gram on p. 84).

Richard W. Krevolin

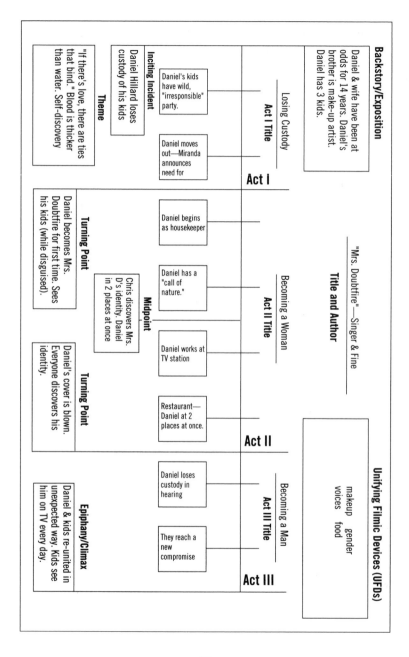

84

Once you fill in all the blank boxes and have a clear picture of the major moments in your movie, the next step involves adding the surrounding scenes that flesh out the story. In order to do this, traditionalists like to use notecards pinned to a corkboard, while many modern day whiz-kids enjoy using post-it notes on their walls. Choose any method that allows you to plot out the course of your story and see the whole picture at once.

Another way to develop your story is to use a step outline or a master scene list, which should include at least fifty major scenes. All these scenes should be essential to furthering the story. Each should have a *raison d'etre*, and there should be some change in the status quo by the end of every scene. And as you journey from scene to scene, think of alternating between zeniths and nadirs, high and low moments, happy and sad, interiors and exteriors. As in dining, where eating a forkful or even a thin slice of cheesecake can thrill the palate and consuming the whole cake in one sitting can be vomit-inducing, so in screenwriting there is a need for moderation. Or here's another way to think of it: Even sex is fine for a few minutes, or God forbid, a few hours; but imagine a day-long session of nonstop copulation, and what was once a pleasure soon becomes a miserable occupation. Yes, there is such a phenomenon as too much of a good thing.

Let me illustrate more specifically by taking you on a structural analysis of a modern classic, *Mrs. Doubtfire*, written by Randi Mayem Singer and Leslie Dixon and directed by Chris Columbus.

: Structural Recap

On the facing page, I have done a complete scene-o-gram of this film for you to refer to as we go. In *Mrs. Doubtfire*, there are forty-eight major scenes over the course of 125 minutes. Within the first ten minutes, we meet all the main characters and learn that the marriage of the Hillards, played by Robin Williams and Sally Field, appears to be over. By the end of the first act, twenty-seven minutes into the film, the need for a housekeeper is announced and Robin Williams responds. He tells his brother to make him into a woman. This is the end of Act I; thirty-three minutes and fourteen scenes have elapsed.

At the beginning of Act II, the Mrs. Doubtfire character appears. There is a series of complications. The main character in drag *discovers things as a woman he could never have discovered as himself.*

Seventy-nine minutes into the film, the Mrs. D. character asks, "What am I doing here? This is beyond obsession." At the end of Act II, the two things Mrs. D. wants most are converging. The tension builds. In a crisis moment, Mrs. D. inadvertently reveals that she is really a he—and her employer's ex-husband. The lie has been revealed for what it is. This is the main character's lowest moment. As Act II ends, seventy-two minutes and twenty-eight major scenes have elapsed since the end of Act I.

One-hundred-six minutes into the film, Act III begins. This act is short and sweet. There are seven major scenes which take nineteen minutes. The couple is reunited, but not in the way we might have anticipated. The surprise ending takes the emotional low and makes it into a high. The final message is delivered on television, where Mrs. D. reads a letter which tells of a little girl whose parents are now separated. Mrs. D. offers advice to the little girl who sent the letter, stating that sometimes parents get back together, sometimes they don't. Either way, they still love their child. This speech is written to affirm and foster acceptance of new forms of families as opposed to the so-called traditional two-parent home. Mrs. D. ends the movie by saying, "If there's love, there are ties that bind.

There will be a family in your heart. All my love, you're gonna be all right."

: Thematic Analysis

The movie ends with a mixed message; it is, at the same time, upbeat and downbeat. The Hillards find a new arrangement that is agreeable to both parties, but it is not the traditional arrangement we would have expected. As in many marriages, Mommy and Daddy do not and cannot get back together, but love does survive. Also, in an age when no one has time to take care of the children, the ultimate image of the perfect caretaker is fulfilled by the nanny (Mrs. Doubtfire) and television. (In fact, it is television which has arisen as the ultimate primary caretaker for a new generation of children.) Finally, Robin Williams' transsexuality serves as a comic take on the difficulty we have with understanding, developing, and reevaluating gender roles.

: Classic Structure

Wow! I've got chills. A classic example of the three-act Aristotelian structure in action. And gee, it works. This form intuitively appeals to us all, as we are inundated with it in all forms of storytelling to the point that we sense something strange if a film does not follow this structure.

What then can we learn about story structure from this fine example? The story really begins with the inciting incident—in this case, the need for a housekeeper—which may even take place before the movie begins. So when you start writing, think to yourself, what launches my story? What is the major piece of action, event, or incident that launches my protagonist on his or her journey? What occurs to upset the balance of this character's life? What forces them to make a compelling choice which will change their life forever? This problem and the character's reaction to it should almost immediately snag the reader or viewer by the throat, and when you have them in your clammy paws, by God, don't let 'em go. Sure, you gotta let them breathe a bit, but don't loosen your grasp until the story is resolved. Then, and only then, should you slowly release them from your grip.

But exactly how do you do this? Well, as the story progresses, we must sense that something important is at stake. In *Stand by Me* (written by Raynold Gideon and Bruce A. Evans and directed by Rob Reiner), we come to see that the story is about more than finding a body and that our heroes are in serious jeopardy if they continue forward. The stakes are constantly being elevated. Their lives are constantly being threatened (by a train, leeches, monsters in the night, Kiefer Sutherland and his thugs) as they journey from one near-death experience to another. The stakes are always high, it always seems that there is no way in hell the characters are going to get out of this one, and the viewer thinks that there is no way in hell that the writer can ever top that last scene. But of course, as the story pushes forward, the heroes do escape and the stakes, much to the wonderment and pleasure of the viewer, have been raised even higher by the writer. The scenes all get nearer and nearer to death, but still, our resourceful heroes find a way to elude the Grim Reaper.

This constant pressing forward is the literal definition of rising action in a story and the primary reason that most adventure stories end in physically high places (in *Batman*, the caped crusader fights the Joker at the climax of the story and of course, at the last possible moment, sends the poor Joker plunging to his death, to be phallically impaled in a fitting and bloody denouement).

We always want more and more tension with less and less predictability, except in something like a romantic comedy where we desire and need to see the ending we expect. In *Sleepless in Seattle*, we want, we need to see the lovers come together at the top of the Empire State Building. This is no surprise. Yet, the film still works because the surprises in the film all revolve around not how the movie is going to end, but more importantly, how the lovers overcome seemingly insurmountable obstacles to get there. Or, in other words, the stakes must be developed so that as the story progresses, the more we want them to get to the Empire State Building and be together, the more it seems that there is no way they will ever get there. This then is the No Way Factor, which must be present all the way up to the story's end. To see if it's present in your script, ask yourself, "Self, have I delayed the inevitable in such a fun, interesting, compelling way that even though it may be inevitable, at this moment, it appears impossible?"

And if the answer is yes, God bless you, for you are well on your way.

: Basic Act Goals

Let's look more closely at how the act structure that we analyzed in *Mrs. Doubtfire* can be extrapolated to apply to all classic stories.

As I mentioned earlier, there are no clear act demarcations in a film except those imposed by me. I am intuitively sensing when these act breaks occur. However, a trained eye will soon come to see that there really is something to this act break thing; act divisions are not as invisible and difficult to discern as you might think. I like to imagine act breaks as similar to the Salvador Dali painting that initially resembles a bowl, and then when you look at it again, you realize it's a face, and then you can never see it as a bowl again.

Now that you are aware that a movie is structured in acts, there is a series of important things you should be cognizant of:

: Act I Goals

1. Hook reader with dramatic problem
2. Include inciting incident
3. Have a galvanizing moment that twists the story in a new direction, forever changing the life of the main character and launching us into . . .

: Act II Goals

1. Build your story. Take stakes established in Act I and raise them even higher. You think it can't get any harder for our hero, but alas, 'tis possible. In addition, the conflicts grow more and more intense.

2. Reverse expectations, which forces your protagonist to take greater risks.

3. More and more interesting obstacles appear to prevent him or her from achieving their goals.

4. Avoid a linear series of scenes. Don't be too talky. Keep a sense of urgency and danger. Yes, the second act is where you can deepen your characters and have revelatory monologues in which they reveal the unplumbed depths of their gorgeous souls, but still, you gotta keep moving forward. Always forward with no fluff, no fat, only lean, muscular prose.

5. Does the dramatic problem now represent something larger than the protagonist's life? If your protagonist fails, so what? SO WHAT? I gotta really care by now. Even though I've had a sixty-four-ounce Diet Pepsi and my bladder is on the verge of bursting, I'm afraid to go the bathroom because I fear I'll miss some-

thing crucial. Keep their swollen bladders glued to the seats and you've won.

6. The protagonist inevitably finds herself worse off at the end of the act than she was at the beginning. She must be at a crisis point. What the hell should my main character do now? The decision affects everything and always leads to . . .

: Act III Goals

1. This act needs to feel like a headlong rush to the finish. There is no room for fluff here.

2. Your climax has to be the biggest moment of your film. You should know your climax before you start writing and write backward. Like a maze, which is easier to navigate if you start at the end and go back to the beginning, the secret to screenwriting is that it's much easier if you know your ending before you start. Let me repeat, most writers need to know where they are going before they go there. Once the end is understood, the story merely becomes a filling in of beats that lead inevitably to this moment. And Lord knows, when you finally get to the climax, it's gotta be damn good!

3. You need a sense of resolution. Loose ends must be tied together. But, the key is to tie them in a way that was not initially anticipated. They're expecting the square knot, give them the bow, then watch 'em laugh and cry as you hang 'em. Even in romantic comedies where we know the lovers will get together and in tragedies where we know the hero will die, you must find an interesting way for the lovers to get together and for the hero to die.

4. Remember, a clear resolution is the outcome of a positive crisis decision which empowers your protagonist to succeed in the climax. Your story must force your protagonist to make the deci-

sion that illustrates their character transformation and provides a stirring example of their emotional growth.

That is all. For now . . .

Thank you and God bless,

Art Structure

Writing Exercise #3:

Your homework involves doing a story analysis of an existing modern film that you can rent at your local video store. Watch it three times. First viewing, for pleasure. Second viewing, list major scenes and time them with your watch. Third viewing, impose turning points and act breaks upon these plot points, then analyze specific aspects of the story in terms of how you believe they speak to us.

7/26/99

Dear Art Structure, Writing Deity:

I hate you. I can no longer enjoy movies. I can no longer focus on the big screen; I'm always looking down at my watch, checking the time, and disturbing my loved ones and anyone else in the vicinity. As the story progresses, it's as if I can see the skeleton underneath the skin. Now I know how Superman must feel, always having X-ray vision and seeing Lois Lane's skeleton instead of her voluptuously fleshy frame.

But back to the job at hand. Act breaks are funny things. Before I met you, I never knew what they were. Now I see them everywhere. It's like a "Where's Waldo" puzzle. Once you find Waldo, you see him popping up everywhere.

Cross-eyed Critter

P.S. I know we've agreed to establish a purely professional relationship, you know, one of two minds meeting on a purely spiritual level, but I gotta have something to work with here. I mean, even if you don't want to alter the image I have of you from a photo taken years ago, how about some family background? I mean, what kind of name is Krevolin? And more important, why did you stop writing? You have this incredible body of work from the thirties and forties and then nothing until the seventies and then, once again by the late eighties, nothing. What's up with that? Fine, you don't have to share a recent photo with me, I can live with that. But I can't understand why someone like you would ever stop writing. This I think you owe me. Please know that I am asking you these things only out of love and respect.

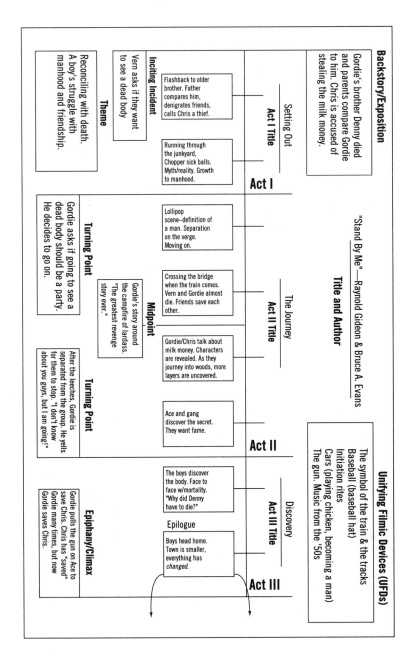

Backstory/Exposition
Gordie's brother Denny died and parents compare Gordie to him. Chris is accused of stealing the milk money.

"Stand By Me"—Raynold Gideon & Bruce A. Evans
Title and Author

Unifying Filmic Devices (UFDs)
The symbol of the train & the tracks
Baseball (baseball hat)
Initiation rites
Cars (playing chicken, becoming a man)
The gun. Music from the '50s

Setting Out
Act I Title

Inciting Incident
Vern asks if they want to see a dead body

Flashback to older brother. Father compares him, denigrates friends, calls Chris a thief.

Running through the junkyard, Chopper sick balls. Myth/reality. Growth to manhood.

Theme
Reconciling with death. A boy's struggle with manhood and friendship.

Act I

The Journey
Act II Title

Lollipop scene–definition of a man. Separation on the verge. Moving on.

Turning Point
Gordie asks if going to see a dead body should be a party. He decides to go on.

Crossing the bridge when the train comes. Vern and Gordie almost die. Friends save each other.

Midpoint
Gordie's story around the campfire of lardass. "The greatest revenge story ever."

Gordie/Chris talk about milk money. Characters are revealed. As they journey into woods, more layers are uncovered.

Turning Point
After the leeches, Gordie is separated from the group. He yells for them to stop. "I don't know about you guys, but I am going!"

Ace and gang discover the secret. They want fame.

Act II

Discovery
Act III Title

The boys discover the body. Face to face w/mortality. "Why did Denny have to die?"

Epilogue

Epiphany/Climax
Gordie pulls the gun on Ace to save Chris. Chris has "saved" Gordie many times, but now Gordie saves Chris.

Boys head home. Town is smaller, everything has *changed.*

Act III

P.P.S. After hearing you rave about it, I decided to do my scene-o-gram of *Stand by Me*. It's enclosed. Enjoy.

P.P.P.S. How much longer are these lessons going to last before I become rich and famous?

8/4/99

Dear Baffy Buck:

First of all, I still write, but I no longer write for public consumption. I write for myself, on yellow legal-sized pads. When these pads are filled, I date them, and throw them in a big cardboard box and never look at them again. This act of keeping a journal makes me happy and is the only type of writing I still enjoy. Furthermore, if you really have so much love and respect for me, you'll understand that at a certain point in his life, the host can get awfully tired of all the parasites sucking the juice out of him. There's a plethora of vampires in this town who make a living by draining the *élan vital* out of artists. After this went on for years, I finally said, "Screw it, let the maggots find another host. I'm dehydrated, toasted, and tired." So I stopped producing new work and soon enough, they went away. Praise the Lord. Amen!

Now my life has become a simple, blessed thing. I live in a small rented house by the Pacific Ocean. I love the smell of the water and the sand. I have a dog, Meshugeneh, who eats all my leftovers. I have an old Toyota Maxima, Athena, that is paid for and fully insured. Every three thousand miles, we Jiffy Lube. The Souplantation offers make-your-own salads (all you can eat, mind you) for $6.95. So, no more chopping veggies for this herbivore. There are several artsy-fartsy movie houses and a bunch of multiplexes all within ten minutes of here. I get in at the senior citizen rate and then sneak around and see two or three movies in an afternoon or evening. I drive Athena onto campus two days a week. I do my thing (I teach, I do not blow my own horn or tell war stories about the golden days when Sammy Goldwyn and I used to blah, blah, blah, yadda, yadda, yadda . . .), I get my paycheck at the end of each month. Once in a while, a residual check appears in the mailbox and I buy a snack for my dog and treat myself to a frozen mochaccino, extra cinnamon (yum-o) after the Souplantation. And at the beginning and end of every day, I sit outside on my small porch and listen to the ebb and flow of the Pacific tide as I read.

Don't laugh. I love it. My whole life, I have always been playing catch-up ball. Stacks of newspapers, magazines, and books have cursed me. Always there, teasing, screaming, "Read me."

"NO, OVER HERE. READ ME!"
"ME FIRST! ME. ME. ME."

And now, thank God, the stacks have disappeared, I hope never to reappear. My *New Yorker* arrives on Thursday and I am finished with it by Friday, unless of course, it is the double fiction issue, which takes a good week. I have two hours every morning for the newspaper. I listen to books on tape in my car. I read novels at night and yes, no stacks, no catching up to do, no fear of someone referring to an article in the *New York Times* at a cocktail party and then, that awful sinking feeling . . .

Yes, I am finally all caught up and well read.

This I find to be the greatest miracle of my life. It's like every day is Sunday without the dread of an encroaching Monday. I can sit under my down comforter, Meshugeneh curled up against me, and lose myself in a great author's mind. The good life . . .

That, my friend, is my rationale and I hope you can understand and respect it.

Now, on to the nitty-gritty. You wanted to know about myths, legends, and their roles in screenwriting, as well as issues of authorial intent. First of all, I don't think you should concern yourself with the issue of authorial intent just right now. Write the story you want to tell and let the critics fight it out among themselves.

Okay, so now let's look at myth and structure. If hypercritical is your middle name, everybody on your block thinks of you as the local Leonard Maltin, and you can dissect a film with the best of them, yet you still feel like there's some deep psychological resonance missing from your work, what should you do? In other words, what are myths exactly and how do you inject your storytelling with a powerful mythological serum?

First of all, the word myth has become a misnomer for something which is not true. For example, "Unicorns don't exist. They're a myth." This is unfortunate, since the most powerful myths tend to represent our truest, most deep-seated fantasies and desires. Myths, the collective dreams of a culture, use the narrative process to link our individual perceptions of the world. Operating on both personal and cultural levels, they are an invisible force that constantly drives us. Think of them as a sea of ideologies in which we are always swimming. Understanding myths will help us explain our lives and provide the stories we need to help us live.

Storytellers have a responsibility to pay attention to the cultural myths and tales of their day. Cultural changes that uses to take decades or centuries to evolve are now happening practically overnight. The world is in massive transition. The new myths of science, medicine, and politics are constantly in flux. Witness the new myths surrounding the spread and treatment of AIDS. Witness the crumbling of Russia and dissolution of the myth of Communism. Witness the lack of faith in the relevance of the myth of a skinny, gentle teacher from Nazareth. In a godless age, new stories are created to take God's place.

We are also ruled by myths on a more personal level. As a child, you are indoctrinated into believing in certain myths: Santa Claus, the Tooth Fairy, parental infallibility. As an adult, you need to become conscious of and explore your own personal mythologies. Why do you act the way you act, believe in certain things, even behave a certain way? These are all invaluable questions that you should answer to grow as a writer and a human being.

Think of it this way: During the course of our lives, we convince ourselves of the validity of certain personal ethos which dominate the way we conduct ourselves. For example, Daddy always said I would never amount to anything, and I have spent my life proving him right. Many students tell me of a schoolteacher who once told them that they were not good writers; as a result, they have internalized this myth, and now it is a part of their own reality that they must overcome if they ever want to feel good about themselves as writers.

So, tell your story. Tell it over and over again, always changing it based upon audience reaction. Find its rhythm. Which details have you winnowed out? Which details keep reappearing, winding themselves through your stories? These are the true and wonderful guideposts that let our lives transcend the mundane to become art. Your job is to put the story out there. As you keep telling your story and it continues to resonate with your audience, it should develop organically. If you have intuitively allowed the story to grow and change, it will tap into your audience's collective psyche and affect them.

Take a moment to consider our successful modern myth makers. Stephen King is able to intuitively sense our fears and articulate them in the form of monsters—material embodiments of our deepest phobias. In doing so, he is making them concrete, real, visual, and perfect for film. Yes, over the course of the story, we are healed by watching the hero triumph over his monsters, which, most importantly, are also representative of our demons.

More specifically, Joseph Campbell stated that myths can be divided into four categories:

1. Myths that relate to the origins of the world and the way the world works;

2. Myths of the human life cycle from birth to death;

3. Myths that explain our relationship to work and other humans;

4. Myths that explain the great mysteries of the cosmos.

Based on these distinctions, we see that there are old *cultural myths* and also present day *cultural realities* that inevitably clash with these myths.

As a result of this clash, we have a space,

CULTURAL MYTHS VS. CULTURAL REALITIES

a gap,
a gulch,
a black hole
that needs to be bridged . . .

For example, you have the worn-out cultural myths that are supposedly ruling our society, the ones that show us the way things are supposed to be, and teach us that, for instance, crime does not pay. This theme is demonstrated in most Westerns and gangster films made before the 1960s, wherein the bad guys get either killed or imprisoned and punished by the end of the film. Then, on the other side of the gap, you have the harsh cultural realities in which people get away with murder, and that drug dealer living in that huge house in the hills is sitting pretty while you've never even jaywalked in your life and you've just been evicted from your tiny little hovel. Thus, a slight discrepancy appears.

Yes, you as a modern day storyteller have the job, the mission, of bridging this gap with your stories. As the poet Pablo Neruda said, capture the empty spaces, "the holes in a fishing net," and fill them with your poetry and art. Write the myths that make us feel better about ourselves, that answer the difficult questions of being alive, that help structure our existence and imbue it with meaning.

Let's look at a hugely successful film—*Forrest Gump*—and how it bridges the myth/reality gap. On one hand, you have the cultural myths, "If you listen to your mother, you will succeed. If you work hard, you will succeed. If you love blindly and monogamously, you will succeed." On the other hand, we all are confronted with the day to day reality that many good people who work hard, listen to their mothers, and love blindly do not succeed. A discrepancy appears.

Never fear, Forrest Gump is here to bridge this gap. Forrest can rewrite our history and in doing so, heal us. Through his simple, innocent perspective, he shows us that we are all simple, good people. He single-handedly makes us feel better about ourselves. Think of him as yuppie Liquid Paper, low-IQ Wite-Out™. After watching this film, we can see Vietnam, Watergate, and all the assassinations of the past thirty years through the eyes of an innocent, and in so doing, eradicate the complexity of our history. We can, in fact, rekindle our sense of American purity and grace. Forrest teaches us the simple lesson that we aren't such bad people; it was just a tough time. And as long as we work hard, listen to Mom, and love blindly, everything will, in the end, work out okay. Trust me. Trust Forrest.

You still aren't convinced? Okay then, take the movie *Home Alone*. This film reconciles the myth that we can leave our children home alone while we work all day and they will be safe, with the reality that every day, children who are left home alone are kidnapped, raped, and killed. Thus, this simple comedy speaks to us all. It appeals to all our latchkey kids who have been left alone and feel insecure about taking care of themselves, and it also speaks to all the parents who have to leave their kids at home alone and worry about their safety. So we can all watch this film and feel less guilty. If I'm a child, I'm empowered; if I'm an adult, my fears are assuaged. Either way, this film makes us feel better about ourselves, and so we spend lotsa moola to see it over and over again and buy the video and all the accompanying merchandise.

So now you no longer have permission to ever say that you don't have anything to write about. Our society is perpetually filled with questions, tensions, problems, topical issues (overpopulation, violence, crime, injustice) which all need to be resolved so that we can live with ourselves and others. When you see injustice, it is your job to create the next Batman or Dirty Harry or "Men in Black" to right the wrongs of an unjust world. When you see a lack of romantic love in our world, it is your job to create the next Harry and Sally to teach us how to love.

In bridging the gap, do we really right the wrongs of society? No, of course not. In most cases, we just enjoy losing ourselves in a newly mythologized cultural reality, if only for two hours. But I believe that by losing reality, if only for a short time, we get an opportunity to glimpse a better world, and ourselves in a better light. And in the end, you can only hope that some greater good may come of these ephemeral glimpses.

The world needs to hear from you. Tell your tale, and your myth will transcend the individual to embody the fears, passions, and desires of the culture as a whole. If you learn to tell your own story, you will also tell the story of all people. And your audience will embrace you.

Class is dismissed, and remember: Even if you sometimes slip into the water, pull yourself back up and keep trying to bridge the gap.

Yours,

Ari Stotle

9/8/99

Dear Ari:

I prostrate myself at your feet and worship your wisdom. It has been invaluable. I am now halfway through my new screenplay, *King Fear,* and it really rocks. Unfortunately, the characters do not seem to be jumping off the page. Any advice?

Your humble servant and scribe,

Play Doh

P.S. Aren't you proud of me? I haven't asked you a single personal question in months.

11/6/99

Dear Play:

Yes, I'm glowing with pride. It is good to see that you are writing and more concerned with your work than my personal life. So now let's get to it. How does one build three-dimensional characters that jump off the page and throttle you?

Very carefully.

But seriously, kiddo, I have a new theory on character construction. Trust me, this one might even be better than "concretizing the abstract." I call it Prof. K's Theory of Scabbing the Wound. In simplest terms, all main characters are wounded souls, and the stories we tell are merely an acting out of the healing process. They are the closing of open wounds, the scabbing-over process.

One of my favorite examples of this is the film *Ordinary People*. In this movie, the psychoanalyst (played by Judd Hirsch) believes that the main character (played by Timothy Hutton) has repressed a memory that is too painful to deal with. Over the course of the film, the act of therapy, of recollection and recovery, culminates in Hutton's discovery of his repressed memory concerning the true nature of his brother's death. This is the character arc of the film, which endows it with Academy Award winning power. The emotional release of Hutton's revelation at the film's climax is a catharsis shared by all audience members.

Another way to think of this arc is that many stories are the acting out of what Freud called the separation and individuation drama. Before birth, we exist in a state of unity and serenity in which all our needs are met. Freud's belief was that once we leave the womb, the rest of our lives is a struggle to return to that gone but not forgotten state of complete security, wholeness, and closure. What I find so interesting about this hypothesis is that these three elements—security, wholeness, and closure—correspond exactly to the basic tenets necessary to achieve the classic Hollywood happy ending.

This being said, you and your characters will be judged not by whether you achieved closure, but by how you and your characters acted over the course of your struggle. We all face the question, How have we gone so far away from home, and how the hell are we gonna get back in one piece?

As Heraclitus said thousands of years ago, "Character is fate," so inherent in who we are is all that has befallen us and all that is going to befall us, both good and bad. When we first meet your main character, her climactic epiphany should already be a peach pit buried deep within her soul, and it is only through a series of events that she, if forced to struggle with her peach pit, is allowed to grow into the fully mature peach tree that has lain dormant within her since we first met her (for more information on this theory of human potential and predeterminism, see James Hillman's brilliant book *The Soul's Code*).

In a nutshell, we care about characters who care deeply about something. It does not matter whether that something is mundane or extraordinary. In *Sixteen Candles*, all Molly Ringwald wants is for somebody, anybody, to remember that she is having her six-teenth birthday. On the opposite hand, my favorite example of a bizarre yet compelling character-desire occurs in *Dog Day Afternoon*, where the main character (played by Al Pacino) holds up a bank to get money for a sex-change operation for his lover. Now, this might not be a good reason for you to hold up a bank, but for him, it is the best reason in the world.

This then is your job: How do you keep your characters con-stantly in conflict as they journey toward closure? What are the obstacles, both inside and outside your characters, that they must face along the way? How much do your characters change in order to get what they want? Keep them uncomfortable and they will expose themselves, and by exposing ourselves and turning ourselves inside out, we grow.

Conflict breeds change.

And change is what the audience desires and needs most for a satisfying filmgoing experience.

: **Structural Aspects of Character Development**

Introduce your main character early in order to set up your dramatic problem. It is only in the second act that the character's full backstory can truly be established. Find a moment when they can have a monologue that reveals the colors and sounds of their soul, their deepest dreams, fears, and secrets. Let them breathe and scream and stink.

By the third act, characters must be fully fleshed out because by now, there is no room for surprises. In the end, characterization is a fraud, and it is up to you to create *believable* frauds. And always, the key to believability is specific details. God is in the details. Be specific. Specific. Specific.

As you write your first draft, you may find that your main character has an initial goal which may turn out in the end to be a false goal. In many cases, it is only over the course of the whole story that the character's true goals are uncovered and achieved. For example, *Stand by Me* at first seems to be a movie about four boys finding a corpse, but by the end we realize that the corpse is just the broomstick engine driving the story. The film is really about one boy confronting and reconciling with the deaths of his older brother and his best friend.

And don't forget the antagonist! This is the character that drives your story and your protagonist forward. The antagonist must be real, natural, believable, yet sure to give the protagonist a run for his or her money. The antagonist must be seemingly more powerful than the protagonist. It is the protagonist who needs to be resourceful and find the means to overcome the antagonist. This is the dynamic give-and-take, the Felix and Oscar Odd Couple Syndrome, the yin and yang, the unity of opposites that Lajos Egris talks about in his classic book *The Art of Dramatic Structure*.

The final factor that makes characters three-dimensional is a certain contradictory-ness or multisidedness; in other words, characters who aren't exactly what they appear to be. For example, in a Christmas episode of the TV series *M*A*S*H*, David Ogden Stiers, who played Major Charles Emerson Winchester, acts pompous and selfish, but by the end of the episode we discover that this is merely a facade masking a humble man who, unbeknownst to everyone including the audience, has been anonymously donating gifts to poor children in the spirit of Christmas.

Whoa, my fingers are throbbing with arthritis, howling for relief. Enough for now.

Prof. K.

P.S. Have you finished that goddamn first draft yet?

Writing Exercise #4:

Describe a colorful, three-dimensional character from your past. Use my patented digital snapshot technique whereby you pick specific moments from your life and visually frame them, fully describing them, coloring them in as if they are glossy digital photographs. Don't forget to employ details to make your character spring to life.

12/11/99

Dear Prof. K.:

Sometimes I feel that you must have known my father. I mean, just like you, he always used to talk about doing stuff to build my character. You know, if this situation would have come up before I met you (I realize we haven't ever really met, but you know what I mean), I would have told you to go fry ice, but I think I'm really growing as a character, so I'll indulge you.

Enjoy,

The Ice Fryer

P.S. I know it's not you, but me. I have a little problem with authority and I'm working on it, okay?

P.P.S. On the following page, you will find some snapshots of my grandfather coupled with a bit of analysis and self-consciousness to properly frame them. I hope this is in accordance with what you expected.

Writing Exercise #4: Digital Snapshots

1. I am eleven years old. It is six o'clock Saturday morning. I am standing in my pajamas in my grandfather's kitchen. White. Shiny white Formica with gold specks. Silver chrome. And appliances from the fifties. In his chair at the head of the table, he is eating a toasted corn muffin with cream cheese. Breakstone's Temp-tee whipped cream cheese. His white, creamy spread of choice. To my grandfather, the downfall of Western civilization,

the decline of mankind, the state of the world could be measured by the price of Temp-tee. I'd hear him tell my mother, "Do you know how much they charge for Temp-tee at Stop 'N Shop? Ninety-five cents. Racketeers . . . thirty-nine cents. I used to pay thirty-nine cents . . . "

2.   After breakfast, we'd get into his Cadillac. This was back when the word Cadillac carried weight. It was the epitome of—LUXURY. Yachtlike. Gargantuan. Gold-toned. With monster-sized tail fins. It smelled of twenty-dollar bills, Vicks cough drops, and wet leather gloves. But the best part about it was, in the center of the back seat there was a thick, cushy armrest that you could pull out and sit on. If you were a kid, it was the best place in the whole car to sit. Better than five phone books piled high, it was a mighty powerful perch, but supple. Soft. Comfy. Shaped exactly right for a five year old's butt. When I sat there, I felt gigantic, strong, important, like a big *macher* (Yiddish for bigshot). Sitting there gave me an appreciation for what it must feel like to be my grandfather.

3.   When we got out of his car, he'd take my small hand in his callused palm and we'd walk down the main street of Terryville toward his huge office in the biggest furniture store in the whole world, the Terryville Furniture Store, which stretched across a vast portion of the downtown Terryville area. A series of white warehouse buildings, it spread out like an enormous cherry blossom in full bloom. And as we walked, I'd always hear people whisper to each other, "That's Harry Simon! He owns the Terryville Furniture Store."

4.   On the way home, as the sun would set and the golden rays would pour in the side windows of the car, I'd sit on my plush throne and ask my grandfather to tell me a story about what his life was like when he was a small boy.

He was five years old. A poverty-stricken child wearing his only pair of woolen knickers. Knees patched over and over again. The material chafing his inner thighs. The dirty rainwater seeping through the holes in his shoes and socks, freezing his feet. His white shirt three sizes too big. The only warm, solid thing in the world was his little sister's hand gripped tightly in his own. His parents gone. Missing. No tears. He will not let himself cry, but he is scared. Cold. So cold.

He is in hiding. If he is discovered, he will be killed. He knows this. He tries not to breathe. To not make a sound. Hiding under the rotting wooden floorboards of his front porch, frightened, watching as Cossacks on horseback storm through his *shtetl* (village), brandishing silver swords, killing men and women, five-year-old boys, destroying homes, setting them on fire, raping, pillaging, engaging in awful, unthinkable deeds as he cowers and prays and the rage grows in him.

The rage gave him the strength to work hard and save money and go to America, where he would not be persecuted for being a Jew. And so, this is not a snapshot of fear, but of emerging strength, for the Cossacks failed in their mission. They didn't realize that they weren't hurting him; they were building his character, endowing him with discipline, power, the force of character to survive and even, to succeed!

12/27/99

Dear Chatchkala:

You're making me proud. I knew you had to be good for something. Now, let's move into the realm of dialogue. Concision is the key here.

What are characters without dialogue?

Silent.

Since *The Jazz Singer*, screen characters have been endowed with the gift of language; they can breathe and swear and scream, but be forewarned: As William Holden said in *Sunset Boulevard*, audiences think that the actors are making up their lines as they go along. And that's what audiences should think—that is of course, if the dialogue is well written. But mark my words—having characters appear as if they are speaking easily is no easy feat. Still, if you understand that writing dialogue is really an exercise in the use of smoke and mirrors, you will be well on your way to achieving Holden's paradigm of writerly invisibility. I refer to smoke because dialogue relies upon hazy misdirection and ambiguity; mirrors, because these smoky shafts of dialogue must be reflected back onto your main character. In order to achieve the ultimate in modern smoke-and-mirror effects, there are several necessary key elements: *Be concise* or $D - 1/3 = 3D$

If you have a choice between saying something in one word or in one sentence, always pick the word. Many times when I read students' scripts, I can eliminate about one-third of the dialogue. In doing so, the scenes become three times better.

Thus, Krev's Dialogue Theorem:

$D - 1/3 = 3D$

I know my theorem looks mathematically impossible, but writing ain't a science, it's an art, and in art, when we carry around our little laminated poetic license, we are allowed certain liberties. So, my friend, please keep it short. Keep it simple. And never forget the ancient Greek epithet: *Brevity is the filet of soul.*

: Use Artifice, But Don't be Artificial

Artifice is our next key element. Or as the great Duke Ellington almost said, "It don't mean a thing, if it don't sound like it sings." For example, if you were to leave a tape recorder on in a booth in a Starbuck's Cafe where two people were eating and then transcribe the dialogue verbatim onto a page, it would not read like good dialogue, even though, yes, it was real (whatever that means). You see, one must focus on the appearance of reality or what is called writing with verisimilitude. Your job as a writer is not to write dialogue that is real; your job is to create dialogue that *sounds as though it is real.* The distinction here—the "sounds as though it is real"—is everything.

: Expository Dialogue

The problem that then arises is that there is usually some vital expository information which, no matter how hard you've tried to convey it visually, ends up having to be spoonfed to the audience through dialogue. Then, when your character articulates the necessary information, it destroys the flow of your script, weighing your story down with awkward, heavy-handed speech.

What is the answer? When you need to include exposition in your dialogue, ensure that it does not sound false by inserting it in scenes rife with extraneous action, conflict, and subtle, off-the-nose techniques. As long as your dialogue is heavy with conflict, it will never become sluggish.

One of my favorite examples of this phenomenon occurs in the recent comedy *Austin Powers: International Man of Mystery*. As in all spy dramas, there is a tremendous amount of expository information that must be given to the audience (usually administered by an audience-surrogate in the film who asks lots of banal questions). The author and star of this comedy, Mike Myers, has the two main characters convey the essential mystery-solving info while he and Elizabeth Hurley are disagreeing. But since this is a comedy, he also has Hurley's character walking around naked, her private parts perfectly covered by Myers' synchronous movements as he does the most British of acts—makes tea. The screenwriter Myers is successful here because as the audience laughs hysterically, they are not aware that they are also being spoonfed the expository information they need to follow the complicated plot.

: Distinctive Character Voices

Remember, each character must have a distinctive voice. In real life, people employ particular jargon and speech patterns that characterize their own perspective. Take the classic sitcom *Seinfeld*; in any *Seinfeld* script, you should be able to grab a random page and know who is speaking.

Let's give it a try: "I'm going to return this peach. This peach is sub-par!" Yep—Kramer.

Or what about, "A cup of coffee, a cup of coffee is not a fix-up. It's not cheating, if there's no sex!" The envelope please . . .

Got to be George Costanza.

: Smoky Shafts of Dialogue

Like good black beans, the best dialogue is always smoky. Dialogue exists between the lines; keep it subtextual and off-the-nose. We should never be able to hear the writer's voice, only the character's. Take the hit men (the John Travolta and Samuel L. Jackson characters) in *Pulp Fiction*. On their way to committing their next murder, they aren't talking about the job, guns, or killing techniques; they're talking about Big Macs and Burger Royales in France. This is wonderful because it reveals the true essences of their characters without dipping into the vast quagmire of clichéd lines that we would usually hear in such a situation. The actors are given lines in which they are able to do what they are paid to do: act. Everything happens between the lines, behind the smoke screen. *Pulp Fiction* jumps off the screen because seemingly ordinary lines are uttered by extraordinary people in extraordinary situations and we never know what's going to be said or happen next.

Audiences love this originality. And to capture it in your dialogue, don't forget that people don't necessarily answer the questions posed to them. In your next screenplay, you might want to try and write a dialogue between your two main characters as two separate monologues woven together; if done properly, the exchange should spring off the page as fresh, original dialogue that seamlessly flows together. Or maybe you want to maintain a sense of discontinuity to demonstrate that, at a certain level, neither of the characters is really listening to the other. Like a good peanut butter and jelly sandwich, you can savor two distinct tastes, but the combination of the two is even better.

The cardinal rule, then, to follow to avoid the pitfall of clichéd lines is, be fearless. Take chances with your dialogue. Audiences have been exposed to thousands of hours of television. They want to hear something new. Try flipping the world around and see what happens. For example, in *Heathers*, the father calls the son "dad" and the son calls the father "son." Or in *Moonstruck*, a moment between Olympia Dukakis as the mother and Cher as her daughter, Loretta, is written as follows:

Mother: Do you love him, Loretta?
Loretta: No.
Mother: Good.

(Betcha didn't expect that answer, huh?)

Earlier in our correspondence, I mentioned that the second or third act is where the main characters and even some of the leading supporting characters usually have what I call a revelatory monologue (a dramatic speech that reveals their innermost feelings). This monologue makes them three-dimensional. For example, think of the classic speech by Fredo (played by John Cazale) in *Godfather II*, "You're my younger brother, Mikey, and I was passed over," or Brando's in *On the Waterfront*, "I could have been a contender. I could have been somebody, instead of a bum, which is what I am." These are powerful, poignant moments that actors covet, audiences never forget, and the Academy Awards people love to use as clips during their big black tie self-celebratory hoo-ha.

Lastly, the more you hear your dialogue read aloud by actors, the more you will develop an ear for fresh and realistic sounding language. In most cases, first drafts contain stilted dialogue that is there only for plot reasons. It's your job during the revision process to make your stilted dialogue sing. Having it read aloud can help. If you can't find any actors, have it read aloud by your friends. If you have no friends, read it out loud to yourself. But, above all, listen to it and you will hear what works. And when you listen, also tune in to what the character does not say. This too, says something and more importantly, it allows the audience to inject themselves into the dialogue and fill in the spaces with their own favorite lines.

This then is the smoke part of this chapter, smoke being the screen behind which the characters' true feelings can be masked. In a powerful scene in Robert Redford's excellent film *Quiz Show*, the antagonist and the main character (Rob Morrow and Ralph Fiennes—pronounced, by the way, Rafe Fines) play poker. Throughout the scene, they speak only of the game at hand, but it soon becomes clear that when they talk about bluffing and calling, they are really speaking about the quiz show scandal in which they are both deeply and inextricably embroiled.

In real life, few people ever express what they really mean. There are a million ways to say I love you without saying the words "I love you!" And in many cases, the other ways are more effective than the direct one. In fact, sometimes the most powerful way to express information is not through dialogue at all but through action. As we already know, actions can speak louder than words. Especially if they are explosions, and we all know how much audiences like things that explode and make lots of noise. So have fun writing your dialogue. Don't become too talky and never forget that the best dialogue is both motivated and restricted by the action of the story.

: **Mirrors**

Now onto the mirrors section of this letter. I say mirrors because a good revelatory monologue should mirror the inner state of the character. Not completely reveal it, for that would contradict our smoke rule, but offer a clear reflection. In addition, many times in scripts, especially at the ends of the second and third acts, there are mirror moments—scenes in which the main character hears or sees another character tell about or go through an experience similar to the one the main character is encountering. For example, toward the end of *Chasing Amy* the main character is having girl problems; it is only after Silent Bob (played by the writer, Kevin Smith) finally speaks and tells the protagonist a story about chasing a girl named Amy that the main character sees himself clearly reflected and figures out what he needs to do. This mirror moment provides a reflection that allows the main character to see his true state of being more clearly, experience an epiphany of sorts, and move forward to do what needs to be done.

: **Components of Good Dialogue**

1. Be concise (D-1/3 = 3D)
2. Use artifice, but don't be artificial
3. Expository dialogue should be buried within scenes rife with conflict and extraneous action
4. A character must have his or her own distinct voice
5. Avoid clichéd speech; keep it fresh
6. Stay smoky, subtle, and subtextual
7. Remember to give some of your characters a good revelatory monologue
8. Use dialogue to mirror your main character's soul.

And never become too talky.

Blah, blah, blah,

The Dialogue Doctor

P.S. Wait a sec, the fun ain't over yet.

Writing Exercise #5:

Your assignment is to write a scene in which one character tries to tell another that he or she loves that person without ever using the "L" word. The scene ends with the object of affection demonstrating through action (and maybe subtle dialogue) that they either accept or reject this love.

P.P.S. Once you have completed this assignment (or if you'd like to try a variation), instead of dealing with love, deal with one person trying to reveal to another that a third party has died. Again, the scene ends with the person to whom the revelation is made responding by either accepting or rejecting the knowledge of the death. Go for it. Make artistic choices that are subtle, ambiguous, and interesting without being vague and incomprehensible.

3/8/00

Dear Dr. D.:

On the following page, please find that I have chosen to write only the love scene, but rest assured, in it are elements of death.

Hope it exceeds your great expectations,

Pip

P.S. I want to send you *King Fear*, but I was wondering if you might elaborate a bit about genres beforehand, because well, I'm not sure if it's a thriller or a horror film or a drama or a black comedy. Help! I have a feeling it needs to fit into one of these categories before I go any further.

Writing Exercise #5: Saying I Love You

INT. JANE'S SUBURBAN HOUSE—NIGHT

JANE, 21, is pacing back and forth. Her brow is wrinkled; she pouts. The doorbell rings.

Jane opens the door. ERIC, 22, stands in the doorway. He holds a weed whacker.

                    ERIC
          I came as soon as I could. Here.

                    JANE
          You're a peach.

She grabs it. Eric enters the foyer and walks straight into the living room.

                    ERIC
    Whacking weeds now, huh?

                    JANE
    The lawn's getting out of control.
    It's very bad. Did you see the—

                    ERIC
    Hello? Three months ago, it was
    my hedge trimmer. Seven months ago,
    my garden hose—

                    JANE
    So sue me if I want to take good
    care of my lawn.

Eric shakes his head in disgust and looks at
his watch.

                    ERIC
    Jose your gardener will be here
    tomorrow mor—

                    JANE
    Yeah, but, I wanted to get a
    head start—

                    ERIC
    He broke up with you, huh?

                    JANE
    Jose? No, he's not my type—

                    ERIC
    Not Jose . . . Teddie!

                    JANE
    Uh-huh. And get this. He did it
    over the phone. Left a message
    on my answering machine.

                    ERIC
    Uhhh! What a cowardly bastard!

She puts the weed whacker down. They both sit.

>   JANE
>   Thanks so much for coming.

>   ERIC
>   No problem . . . So what am I sup-
>   posed to say now? Oh yeah . . .
>   Here goes.
>   (robotic tone)
>   There are other fish in the sea.
>   He doesn't deserve you. I never
>   liked him anyway. You can do much
>   better!
>   (Beat)
>   How was that?

Jane shoots him an angry glare.

>   JANE
>   I thought he was the one. You
>   have no idea what I'm going
>   through right now.

Eric turns away from Jane and starts to chuckle.

>   ERIC
>   God! Are you really that naive?

>   JANE
>   What do you mean? I've seen you
>   at parties. You don't even try.

Eric picks up a magazine off of the coffee table and throws it down.

>   ERIC
>   Oh, bullshit! I'm always trying.
>   I bring over lawn-care products
>   every time you call and I hope
>   (MORE)

                    ERIC (CONT'D)
          and pray that maybe, just maybe
          this time, you'll notice how
          I really feel and I won't have to
          settle for the consolation prize.

                    JANE
          Don't say it, Eric. Please—

He takes her by the hand.

                    ERIC
          I want the brand new Chrysler
          LeBaron convertible. I want the
          four days and three luxurious
          nights in Monte Carlo . . . I'm
          sick of living on Rice-a-Roni.

She understands, pulls her hand away and
stands up.

                    JANE
          Don't worry. You're a very sweet
          boy. I'm sure you'll find someone.

                    ERIC
          Yeah, yeah. Swell. Thanks.

                    JANE
          What do you want me to say?

Eric stands up, but keeps his distance.

                    ERIC
          Never mind. I shouldn't have
          even brought it up.

                    JANE
          Eric, listen. You'll always be
          my best friend in the whole world.

A moment of silence.

> ERIC
>
> Whoopee.

> JANE
>
> Don't. That's not fair.

> ERIC
>
> I know.

Eric grabs his weed whacker.

> ERIC
>
> It's not fair at all . . . Now,
> if you don't mind, I need to
> tend to my own lawn for a while.

Eric turns and walks out. She watches him in silence. A tear drips down her cheek.

FADE OUT.

THE END.

3/20/00

Dear Pip,

Your question about categories is a good one. Yes, storytelling is genre-driven and each genre has demands that must be understood and met. In other words, slow down.

: **Film Genres**

Though precise causal relationships between films and the culture from which they arise are tenuous, films do reflect upon the social, political, and economic atmosphere of the time in which they are produced. And as I wrote in an earlier letter on mythology, those films that reflect most directly (without blinding us, of course) are the ones that the culture ends up embracing. For example, even though many war films deal with conflicts of long ago, they transcend the costume drama genre and stand as covert and sometimes even overt statements about the present American political situation and mood.

Better yet, let us look at sci-fi films such as *Star Trek* and *2001: A Space Odyssey*. The fantastic plots of these films may be occurring during some distant time or in some far-off place, but the impetus of the action conveys pointed comments on the political climate of the present day. As the culture changes, so does the nature of the films made by Hollywood within a genre.

Within any genre, there are many variations; yet there are basic elements that characterize each one. Since there are certain requirements that studio readers and audience members consciously and subconsciously expect to be met, the greater the understanding you have of the genre within which you are working, the greater the chance you have of making a sale. So then, use the following exploration of each of the major genres as a guide to setting your sights before you take aim at your screenplay.

: War Films

War films hold a universal appeal because they depict the most basic of all conflicts—the life-and-death battle of man versus man. Yet the singular importance of war films lies in their visions and revisions of old battles in new light. For example, Stanley Kubrick's riveting masterpiece *Full Metal Jacket* provides a counterbalance to the rash of Vietnam War films (*Apocalypse Now*, *Platoon*, *Rambo*, *Missing in Action*, among others) that preceded and romanticized the horror of it. The first half of Kubrick's film depicts the destruction of the soul of the individual and the dehumanization that war and its machinery breeds. The second half of the film illustrates how the newly bred warriors who are "born to kill" wreak havoc and destruction upon the so-called enemy. Kubrick's film attacks the late seventies—early eighties *Rambo* mentality and demythologizes war without employing *Platoon's* heavy hand.

Another fine example is Ed Zwick's film *Glory*, which represents the work of a modern-day liberal trying his damnedest to rehabilitate the image of the black man in American history. Zwick and screenwriter Kevin Jarre saw the need for a positive portrayal of black soldiers, who have been so important in U.S. military history. They felt that by employing the genre of the historical war melodrama they could redress some of the injustices and false notions of the past that still prevail today. *Glory* works as both an entertaining war film and also as a valiant attempt to force us to reevaluate how we speak of history and race.

:   Comedies

The single most important factor that many aspiring writers tend to overlook is this: Comedies must be funny. This sounds self-evident, but too many writers think that a few clever lines of dialogue or a quirky character make something a comedy, when the reality is that comedy must be based upon an inherently funny premise and brought to life with humorous situations. This being said, you should not forget to have wonderfully funny characters and dialogue, but it is the larger picture that must be funny first.

Let us begin with the comedic premise. My all-time favorite comedic premise belongs to the classic Mel Brooks film *The Producers*. The concept is this: A film producer, played by Zero Mostel, talks to his CPA, played by Gene Wilder, and Mostel comes to realize that if his next play flops, he can keep all the extra investors' funds. So, he wins Wilder over and they go about finding the single worst play in history. They produce it with the worst actors they can find, thereby ensuring that their play will fail and they will be able to pocket all the excess funds. Of course, the brilliance of the premise is that the play is so bad, people think it's good, and instead of a flop, they have a hit on their hands. This conceit is inherently funny, and with the added pleasures of wonderful actors and Brooks' zany dialogue, we have a true comic treasure.

So then, start with the premise. It must allow for wonderfully rich situations where you can mine comic gold. In addition, there is always room for witty dialogue. But the truly big laughs will come from not merely funny lines, but funny lines that come directly from your characters' personalities. For example, the biggest laugh in radio history came from a huge pregnant pause, not even a spoken word. Jack Benny, whose comedic persona was notorious for being stingy, was held up by a gunman who demanded, "Your money or your life!" Benny's genius lay in his timing, his courage to insert a huge pause between the question and his response. When the robber failed to receive an answer, he prodded Benny, "Well, what'll it be?"

Finally Benny answered, "I'm thinking. I'm thinking!"

On paper, funny; delivered with perfect timing on radio, it becomes hysterical.

:   Romantic Comedies

The biggest challenge to writing a romantic comedy is the simple fact that almost everything has been done before. In recent times, it seems as if the best ones have been adventurous enough to find new variations on the traditional theme—boy meets girl, boy loses girl, boy gets girl. Again, we return to premise. How can we vary the premise while still maintaining tension and a conceit that your audience will go along with? In *When Harry Met Sally...*, we deal with the concept of male-female friendships. In *Sleepless in Seattle*, we deal with soulmates who are not allowed to be together until the very end of the film. This leads to tension and comedy.

In *My Best Friend's Wedding*, Julia Roberts has seventy-two hours to prevent the wedding of her best friend, played by Dermot Mulroney—a great filmic premise with a wonderful situation and a built-in ticking clock. Unfortunately, no matter how likable Julia Roberts tends to be, we soon begin to dislike her character since she is acting selfishly and maliciously. However, to the credit of the screenwriter, Ron Bass, he redeems her in the third act and has her act unselfishly. Though this leads to her redemption, it causes a problem for those audience members who don't know what to make of a romantic comedy where the leads are not brought together. As in *Pretty Woman*, where audiences demanded a fairy tale ending (which was added after test screenings), most audiences are inculcated to want Richard Gere or whoever the romantic lead is to sweep them off their feet by the final scene of the film.

So then, your mandate is to find new combinations, twists, and takes, but never to lose sight of the *raison d'etre* of romantic comedies. Love is hard. In many cases, it doesn't work out. If we pay good money to see this type of film, we want the lovers to struggle, we want to think there is no way that they could ever end up together, but in the end, we want them to. We want to see true love conquer all. We need to see Julia get her man (*Pretty Woman*), not give him away (*My Best Friend's Wedding*). We want and need our faith in love to be reaffirmed. Over and over again.

: Science Fiction/Fantasy

Since the *Star Wars* trilogy, the genre of science-fiction/fantasy was misunderstood and underappreciated—that is, until a very fine film called *Stargate* forced studios to think twice. Sure, the *Star Trek* movies have always done well, but films with television backgrounds have built-in audiences and must not be discussed in the same breath as direct-to-the-screen features. As I touched upon earlier, the key to sci-fi and fantasy films is concept, theme, and special effects (f/x). No one would say that *Jurassic Park* is one of the greatest films ever written. But you can't ignore the fact that it is based upon a wonderful conceit (what if dinosaur DNA could be genetically engineered to create living, breathing creatures today?), it is very well-executed both by the writers and director, conveys the theme of science vs. God, and features incredibly cool looking computer-generated images.

We live in an age of technology. Hi-tech films are eye candy that thrills and titillates. Yes, my ticket is expensive; at a cost of just under ten dollars, but I'm getting to participate in a $120 million dollar Dolby, digital, THX, 70-millimeter experience that I would never be able to afford otherwise. If you are a writer that cares about story, the rise of these blockbuster f/x films should trouble you. Yet, as with all titillation, the thrill is short-lived. Once we've seen a specific type of effect, the charm wears off, and the film-maker must revert to the old mainstays—story and character. So, no matter how sophisticated the f/x become, you, the storyteller, will always be needed.

In addition to special effects and concept, I mentioned theme. No matter how far in the past or future the action of our film takes place, or how seemingly fantastic the premise, the theme must be grounded in specific cultural problems of the present day. I would argue that *Independence Day* was so successful because in a world where we find it exceedingly difficult to get along with other nations, the sight of an alien superpower overrunning our world unites us in a common fight and shows us that yes, we can all get along. Or take the *Star Wars* trilogy. *Star Wars* presents a straight-forward struggle where good and evil are clearly defined and read-ily discernible (Luke Skywalker wears white, Darth Vader wears black). So, we see that sci-fi movies are not just about aliens shoot-ing lasers at each other; they must be well-thought-out stories that are considered on all levels—visual effects, story, and theme.

: Gangster Pictures

This genre will always be present, but it has essentially been played out, at least for now. Whatever you write will be compared to the epic *Godfather* trilogy and Martin Scorsese's films. You need to find new variations on the theme. In the thirties and forties, the anti-heroes—Jimmy Cagney, Humphrey Bogart, Robert Mitchum—always received their just deserts and were killed at the end of the picture, proving the theme that crime does not pay (for a wonderful study of the Hollywood antihero or what he calls the outlaw-hero, read Robert B. Ray's *A Certain Tendency of the Hollywood Cinema, 1930–1980*). However, as filmmakers desired to convey more complex and ambiguous messages in the sixties and seventies, they began to complicate their films and the anti-heroes did not always end up six feet under.

: Westerns

It is said that there are only three truly American art forms—Westerns, the blues, and rock and roll. Even though Westerns are grounded in a specific era in our past (the "manifest destiny" expansion of the West, 1865–1910), new Westerns are constantly being made to speak of our society today. For the best study of this phenomenon, read a book by Will Wright called *Sixguns and Society*, which gives a detailed analysis of the Western as a reflection of the changes in American culture over the last century.

As our mores change, so does the nature of our Westerns. As in gangster pictures, the so-called bad guys in Westerns became complex anti-heroes, professionals with whom we empathized and even cheered for to kill the good guys and survive. For example, think of Billy the Kid in *Young Guns* or the lead characters in *Butch Cassidy and the Sundance Kid*. In the post-Vietnam 1970s, Butch and Sundance don't live, yet in the post-Reagan 1990s, Billy the Kid somehow survives. It is up to you to figure out what this means about us as a culture in these two different periods.

: Horror

Ooh! Scare me! Yes, you have to be able to write scenes that scare me so much that I literally have to put the script down and go check and see if the door is locked. In fact, you can study the rules of the updated version of the genre by watching the movie *Scream*. The most successful of all recent horror films, *Scream* was essentially a take-off on this genre in which Wes Craven, the writer-director, played upon the established conventions of the genre (don't answer the phone, don't walk down a dark hall alone, don't have premarital sex, etc.) and had his characters articulate these rules as they killed each other.

The other key to horror films is the villain. Freddy, Chucky, and Jason are all whacked-out psychos who have drawn upon fears buried in our psyches and in doing so, have captured our attention and imaginations.

: Musicals

This form is basically dead. True, there is the occasional exception, such as *Evita*, but even this project was floundering around for years until Madonna came aboard and even then, without the power of the Andrew Lloyd Webber production juggernaut behind it, it would never have seen the light of day (or the darkness of a movie theater). Yet, there are many wonderful old style musical moments in many recent films. These moments can be used comically, as in the opening song and dance sequence from *Austin Powers* or in *The Life of Brian*. So it is important not to ignore the power of music, whether it is in the form of a song playing in the background (*Pretty Woman*), played on the radio by one of your characters (John Cusack in *Say Anything*), sung by one of your characters (Tom Cruise to Kelly McGillis in *Top Gun*), sung in unison by a cast of your characters (*Beetlejuice* or *My Best Friend's Wedding*), or a series of songs used to help define character (ABBA in *Muriel's Wedding*).

Music has become a tremendously significant factor in ticket sales. Sometimes soundtracks get as much as or more recognition than the films they accompany. In fact, in a recent trailer for the video release of *Dead Presidents*, the critic's quote used to advertise the film was not even about the film, but about the soundtrack. So don't hesitate to dictate what type of music or even what specific song should play in your scenes.

: Domestic Melodramas

"Soft" films; character-driven star vehicles. Think *Terms of Endearment* and *Waiting to Exhale* (both of which are based on best-selling books). Formerly called "women's movies," these are being quarantined into the world of cable and made-for-television movies. What makes these films rise above the movie-of-the-week realm is casting. Get Julia Roberts as your lead and all of a sudden your sensitive tale of a boy who gets cancer and dies young is a big-budget feature (especially since her salary is a good ten million dollars). All the studios say they are looking for strong character-driven pieces, but be advised: There is a bias against this type of picture as opposed to the so-called event picture (think *Titanic*). This is based on the blockbuster mentality that has taken Hollywood by storm, wherein executives would rather spend one or two hundred million dollars and pray for a billion return than spend fifteen million for a smaller feature that gives only a thirty million dollar return. (For more information, see "Art House and Independent Films.")

: Action/Adventure

The bread and butter of the spec world. These are the scripts that make agents see dollar signs and repeat the phrase "ker-ching, ker-ching!" Think *Die Hard*, *Die Hard* on a plane (*Air Force One*), *Die Hard* on a bus (*Speed*), on a battleship (*Under Siege*)—basic-ally *Die Hard* anywhere it hasn't been done so far. Now then, the question arises: This type of script can sell for a lot of money and some of these movies make a lot of money—why?

The answer is twofold: Film fans like to see movies over and over again and the market for movies these days is international. First of all, blockbuster films (those that make over one hundred million dollars domestic gross) tend to make this type of money from repeat viewers. People go, they like the movie so much they tell their friends, and they go to see the film again with their friends. Second, much of the money is made overseas, where what counts most is star power (Stallone, Schwarzenegger, Van Damme, Seagal, et al.) and ease of translation.

In essence, this genre, more than all the rest, is based almost completely on visuals. Explosions and car chases play well in any language. In fact, in an interview after the release of *Rambo: First Blood Part II*, Stallone stated that he thought a perfect action film would be one that is purely visual and without dialogue. It is your job to feature chases that have never been seen before and new types of explosions that have never been done before.

: Art House/Independent Films

Essentially lower budget character-driven pieces that do not fit into the Hollywood mold. These are what would inevitably be called "soft films" in development circles. However, these are also called Academy Award-winning films. For example, the Academy's ceremony honoring the best films of 1996 featured a preponderance of these types of films—*Slingblade, The English Patient,* and *Shine,* to name three. Films in this genre are always hard to get made, especially if they aren't based upon a best-selling book. They should be written with the budget in mind. The less costly they are to shoot, the better odds you have of convincing someone to get involved with your project.

Most significantly, this is the genre in which you have the most leeway to say something important about the human condition.

One of my favorite examples is Ingmar Bergman's *The Seventh Seal*. In this film, Bergman confronts the central existential issue of finding meaning in life in the face of certain death. As with Job in the Bible, the task of the hero, Antonius Block (Max Von Sydow) is to discover the answer to this eternal question. In 1957, Ingmar Bergman wrote about what he was trying to do in the program that accompanied the film's release:

> In my film, the Crusader returns from the Crusades as the soldier returns from war today. In the Middle Ages, men lived in terror of the plague. Today they live in fear of the atomic bomb. The Seventh Seal is an allegory with a theme that is quite simple: man, his eternal search for God, with death as his only certainty.

Antonius Block, the Swedish Crusader, is fully aware of his own mortality, especially with the omnipresence of the virulent bubonic plague; yet as the film progresses, Block struggles against death and performs at least one meaningful deed before his demise. In so doing, he endows his otherwise meaningless existence with value. *The Seventh Seal* grapples with this complex problem, and Bergman attempts to rectify or at least assuage this existential dilemma.

Whether or not you agree with Bergman's philosophical take on life, you gotta give the guy credit for thinking deeply about existence and trying to speak of our struggles. The key, though, is not to get too caught up in cerebral concepts. Even Bergman embodied death (concretized the abstract) as the Grim Reaper and, in doing so, avoided the pitfall of making an overly intellectual and boring film. The film is philosophically significant, and just as important, I care about the story and Antonius Block.

: Family Pictures

These used to be called "children's movies," but those marketing geniuses at Disney changed the name to ensure a wider audience than just those under the age of thirteen. Not to be confused with domestic melodramas, family pictures are G-rated comedies or dramas: the sort of picture that Disney was known for and that reached its apogee a few years ago with, for example, *The Lion King*. Warner Bros. had a hit in this genre with *Free Willy*. Unfortunately, since then, most family pictures have not met financial expectations at the box office and the hot market for young people's pictures that crossed over to a general (family) market has seemed to grow cold. Most analysts argue that young people are getting more sophisticated and would rather see PG-13 adult fare such as *Men in Black* than *Hercules* or other G-rated family pics.

Even with the downswing in the market for family pictures, with the rise of video sales and rentals there will always be a need for this type of picture, whether it is live action or animated. Therefore, there are certain components you must include when writing within this genre:

1. The subject can be just about anything as long as it doesn't involve very much vulgar language, realistic violence, or sexual innuendo;

2. There should be a lesson or moral that is conveyed over the course of the action;

3. Don't forget the cute kids and animals, coupled with playfulness and humor.

: **Some Final Thoughts on Genre**

I bumped into a development executive a few years ago, and when we started talking about screenplays, she urged me to consider mixing and matching genres to find new combinations that we have yet to see. Think of how George Lucas conceived of *Star Wars* as a fusion of futuristic sci-fi and old-fashioned Westerns. Just morph Darth Vader's black Stetson into a cool, space-age plastic hood and *voila*, you've got a huge hit! But be careful—too much blending without regard for the inherent requirements of the genres can lead to an unsatisfying mix of something like *Starship Troopers*. Audiences want peanut butter and jelly or peanut butter and marshmallow fluff, but nobody likes jelly and fluff. Sorry.

Hope my generic tirade helped. Now, get cracking.

Your personal taskmaster,

Genre Maven

4/17/00

Dear Slave-driver Whom I Worship and Adore:

I think you just saved me twelve drafts. *King Fear* is definitely a thriller and I have done the work to help it fit within the confines of your clearly defined generic parameters.

Your loving disciple,

The Great Conformist

P.S. As you may have guessed, the first draft of *King Fear* is done and sent under separate cover. Hope it strikes your fancy and doesn't need numerous rewrites.

5/13/00

My Little Conformist:

King Fear is a wonderful read—especially for a first draft. I would never tell you how many drafts to write, but I would recommend a series of rewrites, if not more. You must start to develop the maturity to realize that, yes, there is value to artistic freedom, but film is a collaborative medium and we must engage in the process. And the key to the process is rewriting. I am convinced that the only thing that separates award-winning writers from the rest of us is their ability to rewrite. Everyone's first drafts need work. Great writers know what work needs to be done and spend the hours and days and months and even years necessary to revise their work so that all its many facets shine. They etch and carve and polish it until their work gleams.

But you argue, "C'mon, they're professionals. They all know exactly what to look for." So then, the question becomes, how do you develop the expert vision to see what should be kept in and what should be cut out? The answers lie in an understanding and exploration of the process of revision.

: **Throat-Clearing**

Once upon a time during an (apocryphal?) episode of the now legendary *Newlywed Game*, the host, Bob Eubanks, asked couple number one, "What is your favorite place to make whoopee?"

The young female half of couple number one excitedly hid her card while her new husband said, "The kitchen, Bob!"

The wife smiled and turned her card over to reveal the word, "kitchen." It was a perfect match. They screamed and hugged with joy.

Then Bob Eubanks asked couple number two, "What is your favorite place to make whoopee?"

The young female half of couple number two vibrated with glee as she held her card and waited for her husband's response. She knew the answer and was convinced he knew it as well. Then, he cleared his throat and in a dry monotone, slowly said, "That would be in the butt, Bob. Definitely in the butt!"

In that moment, the male half of couple number two thought his response was correct, appropriate, and sure to lead to a victory and fabulous prizes. However, he soon learned otherwise. The reason I bring this up is simply that many times what seems like a great scene at two o'clock in the morning turns out to be less than great in the light of day.

We all need to do rewrites. No matter how experienced or infamous we may be. I won't venture to say how many drafts we should write before we show a screenplay to Hollywood professionals, but I would recommend doing a series of rewrites. For some, this might mean three drafts, for others thirteen. The first draft is merely throat-clearing, and the characters, themes, and plot are not fully fleshed out until you do a series of other drafts. It is part of the process for us all, no matter how experienced or knowledgeable we may be. Engaging in a series of drafts is not something to be ashamed of, but a natural discipline that one must partake of. The real question that inevitably arises is not how much longer must I keep going, but when should I stop?

Oscar Wilde once said, "Art is never finished, it is merely abandoned." And I think he was right. I don't want to see you turn into Frederick Jackson Turner, sneaking into the Royal Gallery to fix up one of your paintings which you supposedly finished and sold twelve years before. But rest assured, you are a series of drafts away from abandonment or immortalization in the Royal Gallery. So, my dear, lean forward and push.

: **First Drafts**

Anne Lamott in her wonderful book *Bird by Bird* talks about the need for writers to not be afraid of "shitty first drafts." I agree with her. First drafts are about getting the work out there and nothing else. If you are too focused on a perfect first draft, the odds are you will never even finish it. However, instead of thinking of shitty first drafts, I like to encourage my students to write feverish first drafts. Feverish because, like a virus that infects the system, the initial spurt of inspiration causes the body's temperature to rise and then must run its course if it is to be flushed out of the system. Likewise, a first draft must be produced in a feverish delirium or it might never come out at all.

: **Left-Brain versus Right-Brain**

There are two aspects to writing: Call it left-brain/right-brain, call it creating/revising, cerebral/visceral, or mind/heart. Call it any duality that you will, but know that the first draft involves the act of creation. It should be free-form. Let your mind go wild. Do not judge. Avoid the self-censor who paralyzes you. Find your story. Get it all out there. Don't worry, it's just your rough draft. It doesn't count. It's just brainstorming on paper. It's just the beginning, not the end.

Then, after that Oscar Madison, creative, left-brain, feverish first draft has poured out of you, lean in the opposite direction and allow that anal-compulsive, right-brain Felix Unger editor to take over and do his job. Let order become the rule of the day. Develop your rough draft into a highly polished gem of a script. Work it, work it, work it, until it is a thing of beauty.

: **Constructive and Destructive Criticism**

To develop your stories and scripts, at some point you are going to need help from others. These others may be teachers, or other writers, or even paid script consultants. They should be offering constructive, not destructive criticism of your work; this means that they are contributing ideas on how to improve scenes and revealing problems in your script to which you were previously blind, and not just telling you, "This doesn't work . . . for me."

So the point here is, if you are getting help from others, learn to critique your critics. Be especially careful of letting so-called loved ones read your work. Remember to ask yourself: Who is talking? What is his or her agenda? What is yours? Who is the audience for your work? Is your critic part of your audience? Is he or she offering thorns or roses, tainted, wilted lettuce or vitamin-filled spinach that will enrich your story the same way it fills Popeye with strength? Unfortunately, many so-called writing teachers are frustrated never-has-beens who maintain their tenuous authority by pushing aspiring writers down, thereby building themselves up. Or even worse, they are petty, competitive writer wannabes who are jealous of your tenacity and offer mean-spirited criticism in a covert effort to break you down and crucify you.

Hopefully, you can sort through the comments and emerge relatively unscathed. Once you do, pay heed to the criticism that is on the mark. Now that your skin has jelled and thickened to a crusty hardness, it is worth looking at all the criticism one more time. Even if at first you thought some of it was self-serving and wrong-headed, do not misdirect your personal frustrations toward your critic; this is wrong and unfair. If they have taken the time to offer you feedback and it corresponds to other feedback you have received, it is time to stop being defensive and to start the painstakingly hard work of revision.

True, this process is incredibly painful. The only way to numb the hurt is to turn your computer back on and start in on your rewrites. The very act of writing should make you feel a whole lot better. Even though attempts at networking are a significant part of the business, they are not the most important part. Too much time spent away from your writing becomes an act of avoidance. Writing is what you need to do and, in the end, it seems to be the only thing that truly heals.

: Second Drafts and Beyond

With the second draft and beyond, the real work begins. In art as in life, we are judged by the choices we make. Most writers, like most Americans, are created equal; however, as I stated earlier, what separates the writers who get published, produced, and recognized from those who don't is that the published ones have reached a level of self-awareness whereby they intuitively know what to add and what to take out. They'll be the first to tell you that a large percentage of their first drafts are filled with things that don't work; but, fortunately, most published writers have a little something called shame. They are honest enough with themselves to know there are elements of their work which are weak, and they consciously excise these elements until their writing is a series of scenes that do work (their work becomes a series of fresh and original moments that organically flow together).

As in any ball game, when we start, we are all playing on a level field, and the score is zero-zero. Masterful writers have the ability to transcend the field; they know what it takes to score touchdowns. They can see what needs to be done. But they are not really any different than you and I. They are not superhuman; they are merely people who are good at making the right choices. They know when to keep writing and when to stop. Like the kindergarten art teacher who consistently has wonderful fingerpainters in her class because she encourages them to paint whatever they want to yet also knows when to coerce them into stopping before they make a muddy brown mess, you must learn to recognize when your colors are most vivid, and when too much color will serve only to dilute the art.

: **The Polish**

The remaining drafts and the polish require the skills of revising, editing, and re-creating—imposing order upon the disorderly chaos of art. This three-pronged process is involved in every stage of writing, whether you are creating an outline, a scene, a short story, or a full-length script, play, or novel. If the story is dragging, turn up the volume. Ask yourself, what is at stake? And then raise the stakes!

Here are some more questions to ask yourself:

1. Does your antagonist (or antagonists) appear to be stronger than the good guy?

2. Does your main character have a strong arc? Is s/he the type of role an actor is going to want to play?

3. Is it a cliché? Has it been said or done before? If so, STOP!!!! What can you do to make it original or quirky?

4. Do you have a strong climax?

5. Does every scene push the story forward? And does each scene start at the last possible second and end as soon as possible? (In other words, did you get into the scene as late as possible and get out as soon as possible?)

The final draft embodies the union of your creative impulses and the rational structures you have imposed upon them. Think of it as a merger of form and function. Body and soul. Yin and yang. Abbott and Costello. Peanut butter and jelly.

: **Microstories**

Another way to deepen your script is to make sure that it has a microstory in it that echoes the picture's theme. Microstory is a term I coined for any type of tale, parable, allegory, anecdote, myth, or legend told within the context of the larger plot of the film. Not to be confused with a subplot, a microstory usually signifies to the audience what they will be getting from the movie as a whole. Many times microstories are told in pre-credit sequences or by an old, wise character, as in the myth of the horse in *Into the West* or the stories told by the old man and old woman in *Home Alone 1* and *2*. In *Mrs. Doubtfire*, the microstory is the story of modern families as told by Mrs. D. at the very end of the film. In *Stand by Me* it is the barf-a-rama tale, which signifies the empowering ability of storytelling to control and even overcome death. In *To Kill a Mockingbird*, it is the tale of the mockingbird.

If you are having trouble finding your story, microstory, or theme, try talking it out. Hitchcock used to tell the story of the movie he was going to make to everyone he met. This act of telling and retelling your story helps you constantly refine it and determine exactly what your story is about and what you are trying to make it say.

: **Unifying Filmic Devices (UFDs)**

In many scripts there are certain key thematic elements that are repeated and which serve as a sort of author's or auteur's signature; I like to call them unifying filmic devices (UFDs, which should never be confused with UFOs or STDs, please). A box for UFDs appears at the top of the scene-o-gram and is worth keeping in mind. UFDs are not essential to storytelling, but when they are present, they add a level that marks and unites the film. For example, in *Independence Day*, Jeff Goldblum is obsessed with recycling (and by extension, saving the planet), and of course, by the end of the film, he does save the world. Or in *The Graduate*, water imagery serves as the UFD. Ben (Dustin Hoffman) is first seen through a fishtank. His relationship with his parents is symbolized by his efforts to surface out of the pool in his scuba suit and their repeated attempts to push him back in the water, and the climax takes place in a huge glass church that looks like—yep, you guessed it—a large aquarium.

Probably my favorite example of the use of UFDs is by the great director Alfred Hitchcock in his masterpiece *Psycho*. In this film, Hitchcock's composer, Bernard Herrmann, chose to use high-pitched, birdlike screeching in his soundtrack to link the bird imagery with Hitchcock's characterizations. Thus, we have two UFDs working together: birdlike sounds and bird imagery. For example, the opening shot of the film is a bird's-eye view of Phoenix, Arizona, mixed with a romantic musical theme played by stringed instruments. Throughout *Psycho*, Hitchcock mixes bird imagery and harsh birdlike screeching to create fear and confusion in the audience, fear because they anticipate violence when they hear it, and confusion because they associate the bird music with Norman Bates' supposedly homicidal mother even though they should really associate it with Norman, a collector of stuffed birds.

In the famous shower-murder scene, the audience sees Mrs. Bates (Norman in drag) open the shower curtain and then they hear a series of sounds mixed together: first, the curtain rips open, a steam whistle screeches, Janet Leigh screams in terror, the knife stabs her body, and then we hear the now famous high-pitched bird-screeching musical motif played by the string section of the orchestra. As a result of the soundtrack, the audience feels much more terror and also associates the music with Norman, his mother, and the stuffed birds.

The shower scene also refers back to the scene of Janet Leigh driving her car through the pouring rain. In this scene, Hitchcock uses the bird-music motif to add tension. He also focuses his camera on the windshield wiper blades, which look like shiny talons or knives cutting through the water, a direct reference to Norman's knife, which will cut through Janet Leigh's wet body later in the film.

Even the scenery at the Bates Motel is filled with birds—both painted pictures and Norman's stuffed collection. The birds represented in the motel are not joyous birds of flight, but ominous birds of prey. Hitchcock endows these birds with a dark, predatory air, so that upon seeing them, the audience grows tense and scared. Even Norman is shot in dark shadow in such a way that he becomes birdlike in appearance, his nose a beak, his jaws chewing on food like a bird trying to crack open its meal. In fact, in the script, someone comments that Norman eats like a bird, and he responds, "I hear that the expression 'eats like a bird' is a falsity because they really eat a tremendous lot, but I really don't know a lot about birds, I just stuff them."

Norman's comment offers a hint on how we as a society think of birds: On one hand, birds represent beauty and the freedom of flight, yet they also can be destructive, carnivorous forces of nature. This duality is reflected in Norman's schizophrenic behavior; as the psychiatrist explains at the end of the film, two people occupy Norman's brain: a nice looking, well-behaved young man and a predatory, pathological murderer.

Hitchcock and Herrmann skillfully construct a masterpiece of the horror genre by employing a unifying visual motif of birds accompanied by a unifying musical motif of birdlike, screeching music. Together, these elements demonstrate Hitchcock's and Herrmann's genius by affecting the audience more profoundly than either one of these UFDs could have alone.

Now, look at your script, and if you haven't already put at least one UFD into your screenplay, find one and weave it throughout your text. It should add that extra layer which will make the difference between a good read and a good sale.

If you have covered all your bases and abided by the lessons I have mentioned in this and previous letters, you are almost ready to send out your script. And when you do send it out, you get only one chance, so just take it easy there, babe, and keep plugging away.

Zey gezunt,

Prof. K.

P.S. Your homework is to do your rewrite.

8/2/00

Dear Prof. K.:

Thank you so much. Owing to your tutelage, I have finally revised and finished *King Fear*. (Amen!) I am convinced it is the best thing I have ever written. I have sent a copy under separate cover. I am so excited. I know it is the high-concept style of piece that bidding wars are made of.

Hope you enjoy reading it as much as I enjoyed writing it.

All the best,

Ecstatic

9/4/00

Dear Hyper One:

Relax.

I wish I could sing the praises of your little opus and distribute it to all my cronies, but I still don't think it's ready. I hope you have not sent it out anywhere. Go back and read my letter on revisions and keep working at it.

Write back soon,

Trying to help

P.S. As the great Robert Frost said,

We dance round in a ring and suppose,
But the secret sits in the middle and knows.

So kiddo, stop dancing and start sitting.

9/9/00

Dear Wet Blanket,

I'm sorry, but I have to get this off my chest. Are you really try-ing to help, or are you trying to maintain your tenuous authority base by pushing me down and building yourself up? I mean, because you're burned out and have unresolved issues, do you think that justifies your efforts to try to stifle me?

If you haven't already figured it out, I've spent over a year on *King Fear* and frankly, I'm hurt and saddened that you would feel the need to compete with me instead of help me.

I thought you were different, but I guess you're no better than the rest of them.

Outraged and Saddened

9/19/00

Dear Outie:

Until you grow up, I think our correspondence should be discontinued.

Deeply Disappointed

1/1/01

Dear Prof. K.:

Sorry . . .

Sorry, sorry, sorry.

I have been quite depressed and misdirected some of my personal frustrations toward you, which is wrong and unfair. It's just that this whole process is so goddamn painful. I HATE IT!

But then just yesterday, I was reading a biography of T. E. Lawrence (of Arabia) and there was this story about the time he held his hand over a candle and watched the flame singe his skin. When asked if it hurt, T. E. replied, "Yes, but the trick is not to mind."

Ah-ha! That's the trick; I guess I have to learn how not to mind. So now, I've picked my script back up, reevaluated it and I see that, yes, there are still quite a few problems. Okay, fine, yes, you were right.

OKAY! YOU WERE RIGHT! But I'd like you to know that I've started rewriting again and the very act of writing made me feel a whole lot better. I seemed to have forgotten that even though attempts at networking are a significant part of the business, they are not the most important part. Writing is what I do and it seems to be the only thing that truly heals me.

Okay, so how does it feel to hear that? I admit it. I was a bit immature, but can you blame me? It represented over a year's work. I wanted your praise and love, not what at the time appeared to be your further criticism.

Again, I'm sorry.

Repentant and Unworthy

P.S. If this script is ever ready, do you have any recommendations as to the whole business of selling scripts, agents, and the like? I don't need an extensive list, just a few business tips for the layperson. You know, helpful hints from your vast wellspring of knowledge. Any and all clues would be accepted with *mucho gracias.*

Also, what's your take on the history and present reality of Hollywood? Is there any backstory about the movie industry that would be helpful to me?

1/18/01

Dear Kneeling One:

Apology accepted.

As per your request for info about the history and business of screenwriting, here goes nothing, and I mean, nothing.

: History

To truly understand the film business, you should start by looking at its history. In *Film Theory and Criticism*, historian Arthur M. Schlesinger Jr. has estimated that

> In 1937, sixty-one percent of the population went to the movies each week (today it is about 23 percent). The film had for a moment a vital connection with the American emotions—more, I think, than it ever had before; more certainly than it has had since.

The films of the 1930s and 1940s were seen by a huge percentage of the American population. With the rise of TV in the fifties and other forms of mass entertainment in the past few decades, these numbers have kept on dwindling. In fact, David Thomson in an *Esquire* magazine article in August 1977 stated that "over the past seven decades as America's population has doubled, the number of movie tickets sold yearly has fallen by half." The movie industry has been struggling. It wasn't really until 1975 with the release of *Jaws* that things started to change. Essentially, the triumvirate of Steven Spielberg, George Lucas, and Francis Ford Coppola resuscitated the industry. Blockbusters with mega-grosses were the new saviors on the block. In fact, Thomson states that "since 1921, the number of movie tickets sold has risen from 820 million to 1.33 billion." Movies, especially summer and Christmas blockbusters, were back with a vengeance. In order to compete with other media and win back their wandering audience, films had to be bigger, faster, and cooler, with more explosions, death, sex, and special effects than ever before. This is why your small story of three teenagers in a poor mining town isn't getting sold, but they made the futuristic comic book adventure *Judge Dredd*. With this understanding of the marketplace in mind, let us now look at how to jam your script between the frame and the door before it closes on your fingers.

When Joseph Campbell spoke of medieval mythology, he often mentioned that each young knight was compelled to blaze his own path through the forest. This is the key metaphor for each individual's lifelong journey toward a healthy psyche and identity. We each must make our own way through the treacherous Hollywood jungle. Yes, there are some well-trodden trails, but they quickly get overgrown with dense foliage and even if they led to large chunks of gold ore for others before you, there is no guarantee that you will have the same luck. However, the longer you keep searching, blazing new trails, dipping your pan in the river, the better chance you have of coming up with a few nuggets. That is, of course, if you are consistently following your instincts and conscientiously learning from your mistakes, not just methodically and blindly panning the same area over and over again.

: **Shmoozing**

While mixed metaphors such as the previously mentioned trailblazing gold panner can sometimes help clarify the business of screenwriting, the reality of Hollywood is such that sometimes it seems that success is as much about shmoozing as it is about writing. First and foremost, it is always what is on the page that counts, but if a studio executive or an agent has to choose between a shlumpy, antisocial, inarticulate shmuck and a well-groomed, highly articulate type who seems capable and handles him or herself well in meetings, guess who is going to get the writing assignment?

Yep, kiddo, screenwriting is not just an art and a craft, it is also a business. No matter how well you write, you cannot afford to be a pure *artiste*, sitting in your loft, chain-smoking and looking down upon the rest of us with disdain. You have to be able to sell yourself on the page, on the phone, and in person. Once someone likes your script, they have to like you and want to spend hours and hours huddled in a room with you. So guess what? All that work you have done developing yourself as a human being as well as a writer will finally pay off.

: **Getting It Out There**

Let us start at the beginning. A screenplay is truly finished only when it is sold and/or produced, and this will never happen unless you get it out there. The first question which then inevitably arises among novice screenwriters is simply one of snatchery. Yes, I'm talking cold-blooded thievery. The false, illegal and heartless co-option of your work by another (usually an oily, sleazy, and conniving type) without credit or remuneration. Does it really happen? Sure. Does it happen a lot? No. Should it stop you from ever submitting your work? No! What can you do to keep it from happening to you?

You can start by registering your script with the Writers Guild (7000 West 3rd St., Los Angeles, CA 90048, 323-782-4500) and/or the Copyright Office (Library of Congress, Washington, D.C., 20059, 202-707-3000), but alas, kiddo, you can't register ideas, so if you write a great script about a talking zebra, they can change it to a talking giraffe and there's nothing you can do about it except go to the zoo and curse at all the giraffes you meet.

In the end, you have to believe that it's cheaper for them to hire an unknown like you for Writers Guild minimum than to steal your idea and pay a heavy hitter the big bucks to do what you have already done for them at a fraction of the cost. And so, yes, if they ask you to sign a waiver before they read it, you really have no choice but to sign. It's okay; life is full of risks. Your script ain't gonna do anybody any good sitting there on your nightstand collecting cobwebs and coffee stains.

So, go ahead. Live a little. C'mon. Take a chance. Put it out there and pray. Odds are you won't be screwed. And if you are, go away on vacation without your computer, frolic in the water, come home and then write an even better script.

: **Representation**

Now, on to the wacky, wonderful world of agents. It is rumored that years ago, agents would foster young talent. They would take on an unknown based on the possibility that s/he might turn into the next Robert Towne or William Goldman. These days, the agents I meet just don't seem to have the time or energy to do this. They are under the gun to make as much money as possible and maintain their huge client load. All they want are commercially viable scripts that they can sell immediately. It is a game of instant gratification, not long-term artistic growth. So, unless you come highly recommended or already have a track record and representation, they probably won't be interested in you. Thus, the first catch-22 of the Hollywood world: How can I get my script out there if I don't have an agent, when everyone says that I can't get an agent unless I have stuff that is already out there? Badda-bing, badda-boom! Is Hollywood a great town or what?

: **Creating a Certain Sense of Sizzle**

Welcome to La-La Land. I have come to believe that it is almost impossible to get an agent unless they come after you. So then, you must create your own mystique, aura, heat, and sizzle, so when they do stick their noses out and sniff around, you are good and stinky. But how do I create sizzle, you may ask? Well, there is no one correct answer. If you know anyone—a teacher, friend, family member, cousin, distant relative—who is represented, have them make a recommendation and then follow up on it. If this doesn't work, create your own heat by attaching yourself to something that agents might want. This could be anything, no matter where in the world you may live. Make a film and enter it in festivals. Get the rights to a book or a current-event-social-issue type thing that people are fascinated by. And if all else fails, the easiest way to an agent's heart these days is to offer him or her Cuban cigars. However, be careful smuggling them into the country; there's a hefty fine.

Before we go any further, I'd like to stress the fact that to truly understand agents, you need to understand a basic credo upon which almost everything in Hollywood is hinged:

There are only two types of people in this town. Those who create something from nothing (writers) and those who build upon that creation (actors, directors, agents, lawyers, producers, development executives); so the majority of people, no matter how talented they are at doing their jobs, have to attach themselves to those who can create.

Therefore, if you fancy yourself a pure writer (big mistake) one who fantasizes about doing nothing else but staying at home and working, having representation is essential. But beware of this fantasy. You see, representation has its price. If you were to sell a project, here are a few of the people who would get a cut: manager, 15 percent; agent, 10 percent; lawyer, 5 percent; the good old U.S.

Government, 40 percent. What's left for you, the writer? You do the math, Newton.

Now, some sort of representation is necessary, but you must seek it out judiciously. And unfortunately, in most cases, agents and managers are not going to be interested in you until you're successful enough that you don't need them. But if you do get a bite, judge them by their enthusiasm and excitement for your work, and remember: In the end, you are your own number one client, and no one cares about you and your work as much as you do. Most of the work you get will be generated by you, no matter how good your representation may be or how many doors they have opened for you.

Let me give you a more specific example. I bust my hump on a project for two years, sell it for what seems like a lot of money, let's say the whopping sum of $100,000; and after all is said and done, what do I have to show for myself at the end of the day—$30,000 divided by two, which equals $15,000 a year. I could have been making more money flipping burgers at MacWendy's. But, before you give it all up and say, "Screw it, let the maggots find another host. I don't want the vampires sucking the creative juices out of me," be conscious of this potential reality and don't enter the business with cash registers ringing in your ears.

: **Business Practices**

Yes, the agent track is a dubious one filled with pitfalls. However, if you are fortunate enough to reach an agent who accepts unsolicited manuscripts, whether you've made contact over the phone or by letter, send your script, wait a week or two, and then call to see if he or she has received it. Then wait a few more weeks and if you still haven't heard from them, call once a week and ask politely if they have gotten to it yet. More than once a week and you're getting dangerously close to becoming a nuisance. Less than once a week and they might forget about you. If they do express interest, and maybe even, God forbid, sign you, remember, they are not demigods. You still have to keep working on your craft and you are not their only client, so don't stop writing and spend your life sitting around waiting. Make things happen for yourself, and then bring the agent in to help negotiate your deal.

: When All Else Fails, Represent Yourself

Now, if you are running into a brick wall in the agency world, there are alternatives. You are allowed to climb over the agency stepladder and head directly to production companies. Sure, it's slippery, but it's possible. There are several ways to go about it. First of all, there are tons of Hollywood lawyers and managers who are always searching for good scripts to get their paws on and push around town. If they do, rest assured, they will take a commission (a percentage of your fees—lawyers usually get five percent, managers, fifteen) or a producer credit; so make sure you are clear as to the arrangement before you allow them to go out with your project.

Next, there is the *Hollywood Creative Directory* and *The Hollywood Reporter Blue Book*. These handbooks are fairly expensive (they are available at any Samuel French or movie specialty bookstore), and list the phone numbers and contact names for the players at every major studio and many independent production companies. So, if you have written the perfect vehicle for Bette Midler, you can look her up and cold-call her company, All-Girl Productions. Sure, you might get stonewalled, rejected, and humiliated, but these companies always need product for their clients, so there is always a chance that when you call they will ask you to sign a release and send it along with your script. Remember, if you get someone on the phone, you only have a few seconds to try to interest them in your project; so be concise, enthusiastic, and prepared for your few seconds of potential fame.

I'm sure there are also many Web sites for you to explore and many industry people whom you can e-mail. At least this is what my students claim. I am still offline and want to stay that way, but if I were trying to break into the industry today, I would not ignore the 'Net.

Another potential venue is a stroll through your local video store, in which you are urged to pick up titles that are similar to your project. Look at the credits and note the production companies involved. Go back to your resource material and find the names and numbers of the people you might want to talk to. The odds are they won't be interested, but how will you ever know for sure unless you call or write and find out? And please, pace yourself. If you've gotten put off, hung up on, or told to buzz off more than five times in any one hour, stop and start again the following day. But whatever happens, always dedicate a portion of your day, whether it is ten minutes or two hours, to the business of being a professional writer (mailings, phone calls, follow-ups, photocopying, pursuing leads, and the like).

: **Pitching Your Idea**

When you go into your pitch, be upbeat, friendly, cordial. Don't start in by talking about your project. Talk about a movie you've seen recently. Don't be negative. Talk about the Dodgers. Show them you can do more than write and you are interested in other things besides writing. And when you pitch, have tremendous enthusiasm for your project. If you don't, how can you expect them to? Most executives suffer from attention deficit disorder and none seem to have discovered Ritalin, so make it brief and colorful. And if it ain't working, don't push it. Pull in the reins. Throw out another idea. If they're unreceptive, get out when the getting's good. Don't overstay your welcome and don't fret if you get no response.

In the end, people want to work with people they like. Are you difficult? Well then, you won't be working very often. In any and all business relations, choose your fights. Yes, there are times to stand up for what you believe, but film is a commercial, collaborative medium. Never forget this.

Over the years, I have talked to many successful writers and when they are not complaining about how directors and producers have bastardized their work, it seems to me that the common bond among them is a tendency to avoid preciousness in their work. Will it kill you to lose that character or scene or line? Probably not.

An old teacher of mine, screenwriter Stirling Silliphant, Academy Award winner for *In the Heat of the Night* and the first man to be paid a million dollars for a script, once told me that the biggest mistake he ever made was moving to Beverly Hills. He said that once he committed to the big house and the 90210 lifestyle, it destroyed his writing career by forcing him to take assignments for money instead of choosing projects based on his passion. He said that the best advice he could offer an aspiring writer would be to *live simply.* If you want to be happy as a professional writer, you'll want the luxury of choosing projects you believe in instead of being forced to take projects to pay the mortgage.

: Finishing Touches, or the Cherry on Top

The surest sign of an amateur is a spiral-bound script with a fancy cover. Keep it simple. Have a plain cover page with just the necessary info: title, name, date, Writers Guild of America registration number and address. Three-hole punch. Two brass round-headed fasteners. A simple card stock cover on front and back if desired. And please, keep it more than 85 pages and fewer than 130.

Most important, never submit too early. You only get one chance. So when you are finally convinced it is ready to go out, resist the temptation, seal it up in an envelope, stick it in a safety deposit box for a week, and then, after your mandatory seven days have expired, pick it up, reread it, and if you are still convinced it is perfect, yes, please send it out to anyone and everyone you have ever met.

And wait. And wait. And wait . . .

: **Dealing With Rejection**

Most likely, it will get rejected. For most of us, there will be lots of rejection, and times when it gets so bad you'll want to stay in bed for days, draw the curtains, and weep. Times when you will need to just hold yourself, rocking back and forth, back and forth until the sadness finally lifts, and you can once again get out of bed.

Don't worry, this is normal. There is not much else to say. Be open to your growth. Enjoy the daily process. By now you should see that . . . rejection is good.

: **Rejection Is Good**

Yes, rejection is good. The fact that you are not rich and famous yet is good. See rejection not as a snuffing, a stamping out of your soul, but as a rebirth, a gift that forces you to change, to learn, to grow. It is merely the world saying to you, "Sorry, but we will not let you in the door until you are ready. And based upon what we have read, you are not ready. Don't be mad at us, but thank us, because when we finally do let you in, you will be ready to enter."

This is an appeal for you to not take a short-sighted approach to life, art, and screenwriting, and to take the long view. Enjoy the process of writing and rewriting. Many times, we are writing to please someone besides ourselves. This is okay; the desire for parental and tutelary validation and approval is genetically encoded. In the olde days when the childhood death rate was over fifty percent, the prehistoric kiddies who survived were the ones who were well loved by their parents. In other words, those who gained the most approval were the ones who lived long enough to procreate and further the gene pool that one day created you. Yet the really significant question is, what pleases you? What kind of movies do you want to see? Write those films; write for yourself. Then and only then will you be pleasing others, and in turn, they will no longer reject your work.

: **The Hall of Rejection**

If you've tried, really tried to see rejection as something good, yet you've failed and are close to the edge, there's one last little trick that might help: build a Hall of Rejection. Yep, as a young writer, I was rejected on hundreds of occasions (at last count). At first I was miserable, but then I made a conscious choice to embrace rejection by pinning up all my rejection letters in the hall of my house, creating my own personal Hall of Rejection through which I had to pass to get to the bathroom. Soon, I was inured to all the rejections. They no longer held sway over me. In sharing my rejections with family and friends, I took the Devil in my arms, we became fast friends, and my colleagues marveled at my tenacity.

Stick it out, baby!

Prof. K.

3/3/01

Dear Prof. K.:

I'm glad we're friends again, but I have to be honest with you here; this whole filmic writing thing seems way too structured and limiting for me. I've come to believe that Hollywood's a basin of liars filled with plastic, superficial people I can't relate to. I want to spread my wings, soar with poetic language, rise above the hypocrisy of La-La-Land. I want to have the freedom to write scenes that last more than a page. I want to create fully realized dramatic moments filled with real three-dimensional human beings, not just two-dimensional characters.

In other words, no agents, managers, or producers will return my calls or letters, so I'm thinking of moving into fiction or play-writing. Any thoughts?

Best,

Nöel Coward

P.S. Am I crazy? Am I throwing years of hard work into the wind?

4/5/01

Dear Coward:

The wind blows long and hard and what you throw into it tends to come back in your face. So, yes, screenwriting is highly structured and not for everyone. But rest assured, everything I have taught you about screenwriting is not limited to that domain. Good storytelling is not an exclusive thing. You have been given the fundamental narrative skills to work in any medium—theater, fiction, television, it doesn't matter. Tell a good story and you will have an audience. And even if you choose to keep your stories to yourself, the act of writing down your stories may serve as a method of structuring your life.

Okay now. So, you want to talk fiction and theater, let's talk.

: **Novel and Theatrical Alternatives**

Let's start with fiction. It is almost impossible for a new writer to get a full-length work of fiction published. Realistically speaking, you should start with short fiction and submit to any and all literary magazines. As you develop a portfolio of published work, then and probably only then will long form publishing possibilities arise. But even if they do, in most cases, there is not very much money involved, at least compared to the fees paid in the television and film world.

It is a bit easier to get produced in the theater world, and, worst-case scenario, you can always put together a little money and a few actors and produce your own work. But, if you care about making money, don't even start. If you're not capable of collaboration, go back home. If you're afraid of critics, hide in bed. The theater can be the most liberating, exhilarating, soul-enriching, edifying place in the world, but it is never predictable. Nor should you be.

If you care about language, the theater is a good starting point. In the film world, the director is God; in the theater world, thank God, it's the writer. Nobody can change a damn word without your consent. Sure, the actors can screw up your words on stage, but if they're doing it night after night, you have every right to fire them or pull the play.

You also might want to consider the popular trend in theatrical circles these days toward one-person shows. Let me be more specific. Funding for the arts is drying up and shows with small casts are inexpensive to produce; hence, a proliferation of small, inexpensive plays. Yet, if the actors are talented and the writing is strong, they can be very powerful. The theater is the realm of the imagination; there are no rules and nothing is impossible. Venture forth and take chances, for that is what the stage was designed for.

Your favorite playwright,

George Bernard Krevolin

4/14/01

Dear Geo.:

Thanks so much for your diatribe.

Well, as you probably have already guessed, no matter how hard I try to write, in any and all media, I seem to be running into brick walls—head first, no helmet or protective gear whatsoever.

Yep. The truth is simply this—I'm blocked, depressed as hell, and thinking of giving up writing altogether. Nobody in the movie business will call me back. I can't even get a freaking play produced in a shoddy little fifty-seat theater in the crappy part of Hollywood. What I do write is being rejected so often that it's getting harder and harder to create anything of value without wondering if it's just a magnificent waste of time and energy.

At this point, I feel like it's time to quit. Just thought you should know, because in many ways, you started this whole thing. But I don't blame you, I know you meant well.

Depressed as Hell

P.S. Have you heard good things about Prozac?

4/25/01

Dear Blocked One:

Take two Prozac dipped in melted chocolate Ex-Lax and read the rest of this letter tomorrow morning.

(. . . Later . . .)

Welcome back, my friend. And if the Prozac and Ex-Lax didn't work, I pray the rest of this letter will; so sit up straight and listen. The way you are feeling at any given moment is just a function of your brain chemistry, so I hope the following tale will jar your serotonin levels to that post-orgasmic, Ben & Jerry's high that you so dearly need right now.

First, make sure the rent's been paid. Then, sit down with a little *Les Miserables* on the old victrola and a Coke Classic—lots of ice—and focus on the art form. I tell my students that if they can write one good scene a day, or even one good line, then at least their lives have some semblance of meaning. I know it's crazy, like hollering into a cave, Hello . . . *hello* . . . *hello* . . . *hello* . . . with the only answer your own distorted voice repeating the same words. But at least it's a response.

Lest we forget, writing is America's number one pastime, and every shmuck who got through sixth grade thinks he knows how to write; all you gotta do is buy a fancy computer with Microsoft Word, a box of expensive linen paper and an inkjet printer, and you can become a writer. You can just buy your way to becoming an artiste, without any fire or magic in your soul.

What they fail to see is that it doesn't matter how much money you spend, there's no clean and easy way to become a writer. So keep plugging away and avoid hitting the sauce. It'll happen for you, trust me.

Before you go off half-cocked, lie down, pull up your down-filled comforter and listen up—it's storytime.

: **A Yiddish Lesson**

A little old rabbi in Eastern Europe was plagued with a recurring dream about a great treasure buried under a bridge near the king's palace. One day, the village's synagogue burned down and the townspeople desperately needed money to rebuild it. So the rabbi set out to find the buried treasure under the king's bridge. (Please note, since this story takes place before TV existed, people gave more credence to dreams than they do today). The rabbi traveled for days until he finally reached the bridge from his dreams. When he got there, he was told by one of the king's guards that it was against the law to dig on the king's property. The rabbi and the guard argued and since the rabbi was very good at talking (as most rabbis are) the guard soon felt comfortable with him and revealed that he too had been plagued by a recurring dream. However, in his dream, the great treasure was not buried under the king's bridge, but hidden under the stove in a poor old rabbi's house way out in the country. "Ah-ha," said the rabbi, who hugged the guard, and scampered back home. Sure enough, when the rabbi started digging under his stove, he discovered that the treasure he had been searching for was buried under his house the whole time.

Think about it. It was there the whole time. Right under his nose. And so, yes, it is all here for you in L.A. or Topeka or New Haven or Helsinki, or wherever the heck you are, because no matter how far you run, your footprints will always be one step behind you.

: The Caged Tiger Complex

Whether you stay in the theater or come back to screenwriting, sooner or later you will probably come to the conclusion that you and your writer friends really aren't like other people. I like to think of writers as more like a subculture of Kafkaesque hunger-artists, normal in appearance, but really more like starving, wild-eyed caged tigers pacing back and forth.

Yes, writers seem to suffer from the Caged Tiger Complex, whereby they want to be set free from their confines to roam the countryside and become part of the crowd. But even if they do slip through the bars, it's as if everybody else is immediately on to them. No matter how hard the tigers try, everybody can tell that the tigers don't belong, that they don't fit in among *them*. So, we tigers, what do we do? Well, we either wander around, day and night, dreaming of being as ignorantly and blissfully happy as *they* are, or else we panic, run back to the zoo, demand to be let back into our cages, and talk of how completely repulsed we are by the very sight of *them*. Either way, there's never any pleasure in life because we're always too busy thinking about the experience and how we're going to write about it.

So, in the end, we give in to the truth that our cage is the only home we will ever have; it is where we truly belong, pacing back and forth, snarling and snapping at anyone who dares ridicule us.

: The Loneliness of the Long-Form Writer

So now you've worn a path into the concrete floor of your cage, your throat is so sore from growling you want to throw in the towel and pick up and move to someplace new. But moving is not the answer. As I said before, no matter how far you run, your foot-prints will always be one step behind you, as well as all your psychological baggage. So instead of selling the house, get up and look in the mirror.

: **Getting a Life**

Years ago, I had a private student who had been working on her first script for a very long time. She always told me of how she dreamt of selling her screenplay, quitting her bookkeeping job, and becoming a professional writer. Finally, I couldn't help myself. I turned to her and said, "You know, for most people, it takes five to ten scripts (five to ten years, too) before they are writing professional caliber stuff and even then, many of them never make it as professional screenwriters."

She looked at me, drew in a deep breath and said, "I know. And I know I might never sell this. I might never even become a professional writer, and even if I don't, that's okay. I need to write. I love it. It gives me a dream. A life."

So if you ever feel like quitting, if it all feels like a magnificent waste of time and energy, take some time off and think about your dreams and your life.

Do you need to write?

Does it make you a better person? A happier person?

Does it give you a dream? A life?

If you are still unsure, sit up straight and listen to one last story.

: **Trusting the Light Without Going Blind**

Last night as I was driving home, it was drizzling and I drove very slowly. As I turned a corner, I was struck by the specter of the halogen lances of light rushing toward me and receding into the darkness. This image reminded me of when I was sixteen and first learning to drive. I remember shakily drifting down dark country roads in Connecticut only to be horrified by long white spears of light racing toward me. To pierce me. To crash into me. A head-on collision seemed inevitable. Certain death at a young age. I was willing to die, but first, I wanted to fall in love, at least once.

So I pulled over to the side of the road and let the oncoming traffic pass, while my dumbfounded father asked me,

"Why'd you pull over?"
"Dad, they were gonna hit us."
"Ahh. Don't talk crazy!"
"But they were speeding straight at us."

My father touched my hand and said, "Kiddo, take it easy. It just looks that way. All you gotta do is stay on course. Focus on what's in front of you and keep moving forward. Always keep moving forward."

So I did, and miracle of miracles, I passed the oncoming traffic without crashing. I cruised forward in my lane and cars ceaselessly whirred by me in their lane—a good two or three feet separating us. As I moved forward, I started to trust that others would stay in their own lanes as long as I stayed in mine. Yes, I was learning to believe in my own power.

Things looked good. I sped up. No problem. Then suddenly an oncoming vehicle flickered its brights at me as it passed. What was I doing wrong? What was going on? Then, I realized that they were just warning me of a speed trap ahead. I loved the idea that even after my father finished teaching me to drive and I might be driving all alone one night, there would always be others around to warn me, to constantly prove to me that the world can be a hospitable place. Our planet is large, but it is not inherently threatening; it is only the nightly news that convinces us so. Yes, there is much horror and death, but there are also people who drive down the road at night and go out of their way to help others, knowing that there will be no self-gain. Yes, there are well-meaning souls everywhere. There are good folks out there who are trying to protect others and to ease our passage forward. Just stay on course, trusting, traveling, always moving forward.

So let me reach out to you and gently take your hand. Let me comfort you and offer this advice: Stay on course. Focus on what's in front of you and keep moving forward. Always keep moving forward.

There will be times when light will get in your eyes, but the glare doesn't have to blind you. It can be softened with a mere flick of a knob. It can be muted into an ally. It can be transformed into a glowing beacon to guide you on your way. Trust in the light and the flow of the traffic on the road ahead. Trust. As you continue to write, you'll see that all the work you are doing can do only one of two things: Either throw a blanket around you and shroud your world in darkness, or open the curtains and admit more light.

So my dearest friend, as Goethe muttered on his deathbed, choose "more light, more light!"

: **Keep Moving and Be Dogged**

And whatever happens as you keep moving, don't blame other people for being different from you and don't blame Hollywood for being Hollywood. It is a shallow, superficial, capitalistic, consumer-driven place, but it cannot be faulted for being itself. Yes, Oscars happen, but they are freak accidents. Hollywood is not about art, so don't fool yourself and don't blame the denizens of Tinseltown for not being something other than what they are. If you can accept them for who and what they are, then, and only then, should you decide that this is the type of business you want to be in and if these are the types of people you want to play with. There is nothing wrong with commercial writing as long as you understand and appreciate it for what it is: mere commerce, used-word salesmanship, a means for you to amass wealth without breaking your back, a means to exchange your specific skills for desirable goods and services, nothing more or less. And if this sounds a tad too pragmatic, when you can, slip in a highbrow theme or a smidgen of morality when no one's looking.

And if your headlights get blurry or start to fade, remember the three Ps: Patience, Persistence, and Perseverance. As Charlie Darwin used to say, "It's dogged that does it." Be dogged; always keep working. Yes, you will get depressed at times. Yes, you will procrastinate. Yes, there will be bad days when all you write seems trite, clichéd, and hackneyed, but it happens to the best of us.

Never forget—intelligence is relative. How many Einsteins are there really? And if everyone were an Einstein, then who'd be left to watch movies? In fact, Einstein became known as Einstein (instead of Bad Haircut Al, which is what his friends used to call him) once he used his creative intelligence to set himself apart.

All you need to be able to do this is to feel more deeply than the average person, convey that on the page, and be willing to work hard at it. If creativity is defined as the juxtaposition of two seemingly unrelated objects or ideas to create a new object or idea, then try to fashion new metaphors. In doing so, you will be able to reinvent the world and maybe even make a living doing so.

Let's start by reinventing you and giving you a pseudonym, a pen name, a *tabula rasa* upon which to etch. Naming is the creation of self (for more info, see Sting and the Artist Formerly Known as the Symbol Formerly Known as Prince). I'm sure you're aware that I wrote many of my early plays under the *nom de plume* Connecticut Krevolin. I like the alliteration of the hard *k* sound, and getting just the right sounding name is important. Try taking one of the names you used in your letters to me. Or just make up a new pseudonym. If you get confused, think of all the fun God must have had when, after creating all his creatures, he had the chance to name them.

I know of many actors who have faced this problem of naming. An acting teacher friend recommends that her students take their middle names as their first names and use the name of the street they grew up on as their last names. For example, if an actor were named Shana Lynn Smith and she grew up on Locust Road, her stage name would be Lynn Locust. My favorite example of this has to be the story of my friend, Sven Johansen, the Chinese tailor. You see, years ago, when my friend got off the boat at Ellis Island, he was standing in line behind a tall Swedish lumberjack, Sven Johansen. When it was my friend's turn to declare his name, he clearly stated, "Sam Ting." Hence, Sven Johansen, Chinese tailor was born.

Don't fret, don't despair, don't do the Sam Ting as every other frustrated artist who just craps out and tosses in the towel when the going gets a bit rough. Find yourself a new name and start all over. And remember, a little bit of rejection is good for you. It is merely God's way of kicking you in the pants, of saying, as my mother, Evelyn Krevolin used to say, "It's a beautiful day outside, so put that book down and go take a hike!"

Without overburdening my letter with homespun homilies, I'd like to add that no matter how others perceive you and whether they shower you with accolades or apathy, with discipline and hard work you will get better at what you do, and the Artist Formerly Known as You might one day be known as a successful working writer.

I trust you are well on your way.

With only good thoughts and prayers for you,

Connecticut Krevolin

11/7/01

Dear Connecticut Krevolin,

Call me F. X. Holt. I love that name.

I know it's been ages since we last corresponded, but I needed to take a little time off, think, and get my act together. I'm happy to say that I'm writing again, and even though I'll never be able to go to film school full time, I've discovered that there are college extension courses out here where I live. What do you think? It will give me deadlines and contact with other aspiring writers.

Talk to me, babe,

Academically Inclined

12/24/01

Dear Hopeless One,

If you want to take classes, I'm not gonna stop you, but just don't get me started on the academic world.

Okay, you asked for it. I can't resist.

: **Writing Classes**

There comes a time in every screenwriter's career when they feel the need to cease their solitary existence and enroll in a class or workshop. Beware of many of these classes and those who teach them, for the world is filled with petty people. Of course, not all workshops are evil. In fact, there are many wonderful workshops and teachers across the country. Just make sure that the instructor of your workshop promotes constructive, not destructive feedback, and the other students seem talented, supportive, and serious.

With that said and done, I can't resist a little diatribe on the so-called scholarly, academic world. First off, let me preface this by mentioning that due to the financially strapped academic world, this is no longer the age of tenured, chaired faculty, but that of the journeyman teacher, the part-time writer and part-time lecturer who, like the ancient Greek pedant (note the root *ped*—foot—the teachers of yore traveled on foot), travels from one classroom to another to keep bread on his table.

So, my first word of advice to any potential student is to pick your pedant carefully. There are good ones out there, but many are just doing it for the bread. Usually, you can smell these ones from fifty feet away and you should avoid them. If you're unsure of their scent, query them as to whether they're working professionals in their chosen field. If not, there's a good chance they're never-has-beens who want to bring you down before you can achieve more than they did with their miserable, God-forsaken lives.

: **Authorial Intent**

Inevitably, in every class I teach, the following question arises: "All this stuff you talk about, and for that matter, all the stuff that critics and film professors find in a movie, you know, all that subtextual Oedipal stuff and the homoerotic undercurrent type stuff, well, is there any validity to it?

"I mean, let's get real here. We can claim all these post-structural and semiotic phenomena exist within the text; yet, in most cases, if you talk to the writers and directors of these movies, they all seem to echo the same sentiments. 'Oedipal? Homoerotic? Excuse me, but were you dropped on your head as a child?'"

Yes, the majority of filmmakers seem to be completely unaware of most of these phenomena, while critics claim that they are self-evident. Let me give you an example. I once attended a screenwriting seminar taught by Jeff Arch, the guy who wrote the original script for *Sleepless in Seattle*, and afterward I rushed up to him and said, "I read in this scholarly article about your movie that the Empire State Building functions as a rigid, ever-present phallus symbolizing the long, drawn-out sexual tension between the two lovers and their frustrated desire for sexual consummation. Did you have this in mind when you wrote the script?"

At which point, he laughed and said, "Sorry, but sometimes the tip of the Empire State Building is just the tip of the Empire State Building."

So if there is no authorial intent, if the writer and director are not consciously trying to make a movie filled with subtle cultural icons, mythological images, and unifying filmic devices, yet one finds evidence of them within the text anyway, what are we to make of all this? What the hell's an *auteur* anyway? In truth, how conscious are authors? And if authors are unconscious, doesn't that devalue all their hard work and endow every critic, viewer, and audience member with more power than they deserve?

These are all good questions raised over and over again by my students. And the answers are not simple or completely straightforward, but they can and need to be articulated. First of all, the easy question. The French have a theory that has caught on around the world which suggests that the film is so highly influenced by the hand of its director that he or she becomes labeled as the *auteur* (the author) of the film, even if he or she is not the writer.

Now for the more complex inquiries. What we all see as we continue to grow and learn is that the best answers are usually the hardest to come by. Good answers, like good writing, are developed over long periods of time and with great difficulty. The problematic questions of life are not black and white; they exist in that gray matter somewhere between your head and your heart.

The truth is we are all, to a certain extent, unconscious creatures. No matter how much we try to convey certain story elements, inevitably others will reveal themselves to perceptive critics and audience members. Hence, authorial intent is a valid, significant factor, but far from the final word in any analysis of a filmic text. In fact, there is a moment in the film *Annie Hall* that brilliantly deals with this phenomenon. About thirty minutes into the film, there is a scene in which Woody Allen is standing in line to see a movie when a Columbia Film School professor right behind him begins conjecturing on Fellini's authorial intent by paraphrasing the great media theoretician, Marshall McLuhan. Woody gets so annoyed by the professor's pedantic tirade that he reaches behind a nearby curtain and magically pulls out the real Marshall

McLuhan who tells the professor, "You know nothing of my work." This silences the professor and ends any and all debate on McLuhan's authorial intent. Then, Woody turns to the camera and says, "Boy, if life were only like this!"

Yes, we would all love to be able to pull McLuhan out whenever we need him to support our arguments and end all debate. Unfortunately, as Woody admits, life ain't like a Woody Allen film, McLuhan isn't available behind a nearby curtain and authorial intent is a complex and murky issue. There are, however, ways for an author to empower him- or herself.

: **Authorial Empowerment**

First, many writers like to try to layer their work with as much meaning and as many subtle, esoteric references as possible, but never lose sight of the fact that these come second, after telling a good story. If an astute critic notices that in all your work, your characters tend to partake of passionate love affairs with their mothers, you might head back into therapy or move out of your parents' house. Either way, learn from the trends in your work, and then forget about them. If critics find something significant in your text that endows it with greater import and meaning, agree that you meant to put it there (even if you didn't), and if they insist on taking petty potshots at you which could impair your growth as a writer, ignore them. It is not your concern whether the Oedipal impulse shines through clearly; you must concern yourself only with trying to tell the most interesting, original, and vibrant story you can. Period.

: **The Condo-Minimization of America**

Now, as I reflect upon this moment in time wherein the United States comprises less than five percent of the world's population yet consumes more than thirty percent of its resources, and the average American can choose between more than 200 kinds of breakfast cereal yet doesn't know when the Civil War took place, there seems to be a single dominant issue which, above all others, remains un-addressed. It is a phenomenon that I have come to call the mass victimization of America's citizenry. Yes, with the rise of multiculturalism, minority empowerment, and the self-esteem movement, we have also spawned a corresponding rise in competing ethnic victimhoods wherein each minority claims a higher moral ground than the others as a result of greater suffering. This, like other cultural trends, is not readily visible and must be considered carefully.

Let me apply this to the academic world. Twice a week, I walk through the USC commons and see African American kids sitting at one table, Jewish (Jewish American?) kids at another, etc. Yes, students should be free to mix with whomever they like, but of all places, the university should be the one place more than any other where all types of people can learn from and mingle with others.

I am not denigrating the rise of specialty departments (Judaic Studies, African American Studies, Women's Studies), but when so many of the Jewish kids are Judaic Studies majors, so many of the African Americans are African American studies majors, and there are no men taking Women's Studies classes (except of course, that one desperate nerd trying to get laid), why the hell should we have a liberal arts university in the first place?

Worst of all among students today is the rise of a profound sense of self-entitlement, which is undeserved in most cases and seems to me to have arisen directly out of the self-esteem movement. In the name of fostering self-esteem, there is now a whole generation of whiny complainers who challenge their instructors if they receive a B-plus, which is a damned good grade. Think about it—if everyone were to get an A, then wouldn't an A become meaningless? If you ask me, I think it's good to get a C sometimes. I got my share of Cs and look how well I turned out.

I like to think of all this *chazerai* (Yiddish for craziness) as the mass condo-minimization of America, and I'm not talking about two bedroom townhouses here. I use the phrase mass condo-minimization because, like the omnipresent condos that subdivide us from ourselves and like that other modern bane, the personal computer, which succeeds in furthering progress while isolating us from others, we have been condo-minimized.

We all may be living on the same block of this little global village, yet we pass each other without saying hello or even having the social skills to do so. It's as if no matter how hard we try to fuse together the last remaining shards of the great American melting pot, we are inevitably presented with a scratched and dented American salad bowl filled with stale croutons and tasteless low-cal dressing. The minimalist credo of the modernists, "Less is more," no longer seems to apply. These days, less seems like, well, even less.

But we must not settle less, for a stale, wilted salad. The university must remain open and open-minded. It is one of the most important places for free speech and even if disagreements arise, the grappling for truth is worthwhile in and of itself.

: Patience, Persistence, and Perseverance

Thank you for allowing me to get that off my chest. Now, back to writing workshops. In any of these educational situations, there is always the potential for students to become pasteurized, homogenized Syd Field clones, debilitated by criticism, their hearts set on that just-out-of-reach million-dollar spec-script sale. But with an awareness of this potential, you will not fall into this trap, you will take what good you can get out of these classes, and devote your energy to working on a new script, or even better yet, achieving a deeper understanding of yourself.

For only through self-knowledge and cognitive development comes growth. I have seen it in my writing classes. Some students, who may be quite talented in their use of the language, write the same stories over and over again, spinning their wheels, never getting beyond writing that, in its vainglorious effort to display intelligence, succeeds only in demonstrating an irritatingly glib and arch persona. Meanwhile, there's always a quiet young woman in the corner who hasn't spoken much all semester until on the last day, she surprises the dickens out of me with an insightful, bold piece of writing even though her first piece of the semester was a trite sci-fi thriller about a bowl of rancid potato salad gone on a rampage. Or better yet, years later, that acne-scarred dead-head who wrote almost exclusively about giant killer insects all semester finally writes about something real in his own life and he ends up selling his script for a cool million.

: **Beyond Classes**

The path itself is the goal, or as Shakespeare said, "The play is the thing." Life happens while you're grappling with becoming someone or something else.

So keep grappling.

All the Ps on Earth,

Prof. K.

6/2/02

Dear Prof. K.:

Again, sorry for taking so long to get back to you, but I've been writing so much recently, I've been remiss in keeping up with the other aspects of my life.

In keeping with your wise words, I've made art out of my suffering. I thought you might get a kick out of it.

HOW TO BE A SCREENWRITER

Kill your whole family
Or at least disown them.
Write a movie about your parents' divorce
And how they abused you
Sexually and/or emotionally
(before you killed them),
and how you'll never get over it.
(If they didn't get divorced
and/or abuse you,
don't ever tell anyone
and pretend like they did.)
Wear black.
Remember, pain is good.
Find ways to suffer
that look and sound bad
but really aren't.
Don't ever fall in love.
EVER.
Instead, be chaste
and brag about how long it's been.

If you do fall in love,
It must be with someone inaccessible
Who could never love you,
and then write a screenplay about it
Stressing the tragic elements.
Don't forget to fill the pages
with overblown words
From the thesaurus you got for graduation.
If this fails,
Obsess over past relationships
that couldabeen.
Talk about screenwriting
but
Don't really do it.
When you're not talking about screenwriting,
Talk about how much you drink.
Never mention that your gin and tonic
is really just mineral water with a twist.
Xerox every screenplay
you've ever written
For your archives
Which, right now, is an old box
In the basement of your cousin's house
Never look in this box
but feel good about storing your life
In a safe place.
Eat Kraft macaroni and cheese,
Frosted Flakes, Vitamin C, Slim-Fast,
Lime green Jell-o, and red Gummy Bears.
Sleep all the time.
And then, nap in between.

Fantasize about suicide.
Tell everyone
but
know deep down that
it's way too painful
and sloppy so
nap instead.
Avoid other people who wear black
Unless they are as pale as death.
Then talk to them about screenwriting
and drinking and sleeping,
and never ask to see their screenplays,
and never show them yours, either.
Be a semifinalist in
a small, irrelevant screenwriting contest
that pays you nothing.
Then Xerox your award-winning screenplay
and send it to
all the people you hated in your old
stupidgoddamnwritersworkshops.
Don't forget to
Write a poem cynically looking down
upon the writing of screenplays.
Start writing a new screenplay.

There you have it. My first foray into poetry. It's certainly liberating. At least it's short. I hope you like it. My thoughts are with you,

Poetic Soul

7/7/02

Dear T. S. Eliot:

It's good to see that you won't be spending your life wandering the aisles of Borders Books, your mind clouded with puddles of charcoal-black espresso, your tongue filled with tales of suffering and woe, your fingers so badly cramped from holding those Styrofoam cups that you fear you may never be able to pick up a pen again. But, and I mean this, it is easy to get jaded (and you're talking to the King of Jaded here) and being cynical is not a very becoming quality, especially in someone of your youth.

In the end, don't write for your professor, your classmates, or for the critics, write for yourself and for all the so-called underachievers, gangstas, freaks, tabloid readers, tattooed and pierced grunge-rockers, mutants, and nerds; write for any of us who at one time or other in our petty lives ever felt lost, confused, overlooked, left out, or underappreciated, because they are the ones who need you.

For no matter how hard they try to deny it, they are America's real future—the romantics who have the imagination to foster real change, to make the world a more livable, a mo' better place. If only you write for them, who knows? You might end up inspiring one of them to get out from in front of the catatonia-inducing boob tube and, God forbid, crack open a book or maybe even write something themselves.

Think about it.

Trying to help,

Your Hero

12/6/02

Dear Prof. K.:

OHMYGOD! You're not gonna believe this, but I got my movie optioned. They're not giving me a lot. Well, it's a free option actually, but still, the producer seems very gung-ho and I think it's really gonna get made. Thanks for your guidance and help. You're the best. Don't worry, when I become rich and famous, I won't forget you.

Love and best fishes,

The Mogul

P.S. Oh yeah, I know what I said awhile back about giving up screenplays, and I meant it. So, here's what happened. It's kind of weird. Instead of writing, I've been drinking a lot (that's not the weird part). The weird part is that I was at this bar a few weeks ago and I met someone whose next-door neighbor has a sister who is an assistant to this big independent movie producer and so I gave her my script and next thing I knew, BOOM!

12/25/02

Dearest Wunderkind:

Congratulations and all the best of luck in the film world. I hope your movie wins many awards and you are showered with accolades. All your hard work has finally paid off and I'm incredibly proud of you.

Your biggest fan,

Prof. K.

P.S. I want specifics. Write me back and tell me everything.

1/26/03

Dear Prof. K.:

You want to know everything. Okay, I'll tell you. The so-called big independent producer who optioned my script was a shyster, an alcoholic, a liar, a pedophile, and those are his positive attributes.

Sorry, but I don't want to talk about it any more, okay?

Either way, thanks for your advice, support, and kindness. You know, now I can honestly say that I no longer feel aspiring or youthful.

Your friend and mine,

Dazed and Confused

P.S. Sorry I haven't written back sooner, but frankly, I'm depressed as hell! Is my career stalling because I don't live in L.A.? In other words, do I need to live in L.A. to be a real screenwriter? I'd move there, but I've got family and a job here and, well, I can't just up and leave, and, even if I could—the honest truth is I hate L.A.! Do you think this is a problem? Please help!

2/2/03

Dear Old and Expiring:

Just because your movie didn't happen doesn't mean you have to give it all up. Heck, what if it were made and the reviews were bad or it was a box office failure? Neither of these would make *you* a failure as a person or as a writer.

All you can do is this. Put your stuff out there and go home and write some more. Do what you need to do for your own sanity and happiness. Care about what others think but don't be a slave to their opinions, because no matter what they say, it is your piece, not theirs. Go back to your computer and sit, bathed in its phosphorescent glow, safe and happy doing what you do best. Write, and that is enough.

Now, if you are serious about screenwriting, living in L.A. is pretty helpful. It is hard for agents and the like to take you seriously if you are not local; however, many people have sold a script from Bumluck, U.S.A., or moved to L.A., established themselves, and then moved away. For example, take Todd Solondz, a young writer-director who had every screenwriter's dream come true—a signed, three-picture development deal. But he hated L.A., gave it all up, escaped back to his childhood home in New Jersey, and got a real job. But, as you would say, the weird part of this story is that out of this prodigal son's return to the suburban heartland just off the Jersey Pike, we've been graced with *Welcome to the Dollhouse*, a rare breed of film which is unrelentingly brutal and wonderfully funny. We're talking funny in a dark, dark, dark black vein. Have you seen this film? It's so dark, you'll need to turn on your high beams just to see it. I mean, this movie is so dark it makes a drunken weekend with a syphilitic Friedrich Nietzsche look like a twelve-hour Barney video marathon. And unlike most standard Hollywood fare, this one never gives in and lightens up. No happy Hollywood Capra ending here. Think of it this way: What if *Saved by the Bell* were directed by Ingmar Bergman right after his second divorce?

Sorry for that little tirade, but it was just so goddamn refreshing to see an honest movie for once. Now, as to your plight, what do you want me to say—"You're doing all the right things and everything's going to be okay?"

Sorry Charlie, but even if I could say this (which I can't), what difference would it make? In the end, it all starts and finishes with you. You're the one who has to wake up and look at yourself in the mirror every morning when you brush down that cowlick. And when you peer deep into your soulful eyes, what do you see? Respect that image. Listen to that voice. Face the fact that making a living in the arts is nearly impossible.

So go out there and get a job that fulfills the spiritual needs of your soul. Keep writing, but write for yourself and not others, so that their rejection no longer affects your self-esteem. Do not give them that power. It is yours to withhold. Keep writing. It will get you through this darkness. Trust me. If you keep at it, you will get better, and soon the lemmings will be jumping onto the bandwagon to sing your praises and claim that they knew you when. As will I . . .

Only the best,

Your biggest fan

8/18/03

Dear Biggie:

I went on a spiritual retreat last week. Even if I don't live in California, I can try to be earthy-crunchy, can't I?

So, let me tell you all about it. It's called a *lament* and it's based upon the lamentation ritual of the Lakota Sioux people. Essentially, it's an initiation in which a person sits alone in the woods for twenty-four hours. Yep, I paid five hundred goddamn dollars to sit alone in the woods. You're not allowed to eat or drink, thereby cleansing your colon, your soul, and inducing hallucinatory visions, which you must then perform on Earth for all people to see. In other words, you can change the world, but first you need to be produced.

Unfortunately, instead of having cool visions, all I kept thinking about was what I was going to say to you in this letter, and since I was so busy thinking about what I was going to say, I didn't have much of an experience at all.

But two major revelations came from my experience. One, the knowledge that I still have a lot of work left to do if I want to earn my name. Native Americans are not given names at birth, but earn them as a result of a significant event. The other revelation was that I like staying home and writing a lot more than being cold, hungry, and lonely out in the woods.

I hate you. You're right again.

Spiritually Satiated, for now,

Dances with Words

P.S. Have you ever done any crazy stuff like lamenting?

8/28/03

Dear Dances with Words:

Love the new name, but no, I am not a spiritual seeker. I have a bad back and hate camping.

As Marcel Proust said, "The voyage of discovery is not in seeing new landscapes, but in having new eyes." So you don't have to go on any more of these lamentations or fly to India; all your lessons and all your teachers are right in front of you. You just need to have new eyes to see them. Rejections are blessings; difficulties, spiritual stepping-stones. Like a tourist who first enters a new city, look upon the world with wonder. When you do, you will see that Hollywood (whether you live there or are just visiting) is your guru and you must become your own Buddha.

William James in his book *The Varieties of Religious Experience* defined religion as "the attempt to be in harmony with an unseen order of things." So I'm urging you to find harmony in the religion of creativity. All you need resides in your heart, your soul, and your fingers as they glide across the keyboard.

When in doubt, think of the Zen monk who, upon coming home and discovering that he had been robbed of all his earthly possessions, seemed ecstatic. When asked why he was so happy, the monk replied, "The robbers forgot to take the moon out of my window."

So now, dear heart, keep the moon in your window and don't go joining some cult on me. I don't want to see you on the corner of Wilshire and San Vicente hustling roses for a dollar a stem. Speaking of flowers, I have come to see you as my last seed, a tiny acorn planted in a sandy patch of dry crabgrass. So don't shrivel up on me now, kiddo; you must grow big and strong no matter where you choose to take root. You are my only hope for the future.

Best,

The Frugal Gardener

9/8/03

Dear Frugal Gardener:

I'm growing as fast as I can, but hey, thanks for the water.

Now c'mon, be honest here. You must have traveled down an alternative spiritual path at least once way back in the sixties. I mean, didn't everybody back then? Tell me more, tell me more.

I remain,

Dying to Know

P.S. At least tell me a little something personal. Please?

10/9/03

Dear Dying:

Okay, fine! Since you've made it this far and frankly, there's no one else left alive who'll talk to me, I figure I might as well come clean. I was a Hollywood sex symbol in the 1940s. Think Betty Grable's legs and Veronica Lake's face. But I had an awful run-in with a Beverly Hills plastic surgeon who turned me into a crotchety old Jewish man who now has Philip Roth's legs, Jackie Mason's stomach, Carl Reiner's hairline, and Don Knotts' rugged good looks.

I hope this straightens everything out. Love to hear back from you soon.

Love and knishes,

Professor K.

11/2/03

Dearest Prof. K.:

How can I get this plastic surgeon's address?

Contact me ASAP,

Ready for a Change

P.S. Tell me about your family. Do you have a wife or children or any stuff like that?

12/14/03

Dearest Ready One:

What can I tell you? I'm a lonely old fart who doesn't have any family except for my dog, Meshugeneh. I think the only thing I'm good for anymore is worn out tirades against the system and tidbits of writing advice. Let me tell you, the old adage "With age comes wisdom" is hogwash. With age come wrinkles and hair growth out of your ears.

For example, just last night, I dreamed I was so old that while I was sleeping, a cop came by and outlined my body in chalk. The point is many adults are not grown-ups. Most people are as scared, confused, and insecure as you are. So now that you have been informed of this fact, don't just grow older; instead, strive to become a fully formed, mature, responsible grown-up person. But enough about aging. Let's talk about the good stuff.

For many years, I was married to a wonderful woman. Unfortunately, she's been gone for a while now and we've no children—that I know of.

Even though she's passed away, I keep having this dream about her. It goes something like this:

I'm sailing with my wife on our new, slick black speedboat. We've hired a captain to take care of the boat and navigate our trips. It's a clear day. Light breeze. Beautiful. We're cruising to Catalina. If you look ahead, you can see the island, just out to sea, but still far enough away that it will take forty-five minutes to reach it.

We're crashing against the waves. Slapping against the water, my wife is smiling as the salty air blows back her jet-black hair. Then, suddenly, we hit a big wave and my wife is thrown overboard. I scream. I beg the captain to stop, but he won't. The captain doesn't hear me. He just remains motionless, his back to me, his broad, white-jacketed shoulders strong and unmoving.

Then, the captain speeds up and I'm flung against the hard fiberglass of the starboard side. I cling to the rail, holding on for dear life. I look back for my wife and see her floating in our wake, her head bobbing in the water. And there next to her, I see my parents' faces, all my brothers and sisters, like little buoys bobbing around in the water, tossed aside by our white foamy wake.

I want to stop, to turn around, to go back and pick them up, but no matter how loud I yell, the captain doesn't hear me. He just keeps gunning the motor louder and louder. He won't stop. Can't stop.

I see my wife's right hand waving above her head. I scream for her as she floats farther and farther away. At first, it looks like she's waving good-bye, but then I realize she's trying to signal to me for help because she's drowning, dying. My wife, my family, my friends—they're all drowning in the deep blue sea.

I scream at the captain. I holler. I beg, but the captain won't stop for them. The waves, the water, the speed, the captain, it's all happening too fast, so I clench the rail and puke my guts out.

"Please stop. Please. I want to get off."

The captain never turns around. I never see his face, but I can hear him laughing and repeating over and over again, *"Can't stop now. Can't stop now . . . "*

So I just hold on and throw up. Hold on and throw up. Hold on and throw up . . .

I need to make myself feel better, to say something that will make everything okay.

I slowly pull myself forward, dry heaves racking my frame. Always moving forward, inch by inch, until finally I reach him.

The captain. He never even acknowledges me. He just keeps steering the boat, oblivious to the world around him. I can't take it anymore. I grab his shoulder, twist him around, look into his eyes, and I see that they're my eyes. He has my face.

I am the captain.

And I wake up, weeping.

Your Friend

1/4/04

Dear Friend:

I want to thank you so much for sharing some of your personal life with me. For years, I felt as if I knew you, but also that I didn't. I hope that doesn't sound too weird, but it's the truth.

So, of course, now, I want more. More. MORE. MORE!!! Where were you born? On what day? In what year? What's your favorite color, number, football team, and food? I want to know everything about you, but most importantly, if you were younger and you could do it all over again, what would you do? Would you change anything? Would you still be a writer?

Desperate for a Response,

Your Honey Child

P.S. My career is taking off. There is interest in *King Fear*. In fact, I feel like it's almost as if I'm creating a little buzz and gaining a certain sense of sizzle. I have a big pitch meeting at a major production company that has a three-picture deal with Fox next week. Any words of wisdom on the pitch, chief?

P.P.S. I was really hoping there'd be a chance we could have lunch or at least I could see you for a few minutes. Tell me what you think.

1/7/04

My Dearest Pooh Bear:

You keep wanting to meet me and probing for more and more personal information about me, as if greater knowledge of my background will somehow shed more light on who I am. What you fail to see, dear heart, is simply that, as Kafka said, "I consist of literature and am nothing more." At first, this may sound like a copout, but hear me out. It doesn't matter where I was born or how old I am or how much hair I have left. All that is mere poppycock and folderol.

Whether we ever get a chance to see each other or not is irrelevant. You already have seen the best of me. I consist of literature. Reread my letters and you need nothing else. You have my words, my advice, my love in the form of sentences dedicated to your well-being. Don't ask for anything more, for anything else I may give you is mere frosting; it is dressing, shiny gold-plated accessories. You know me better than anyone left on this planet. You have been privy to the special insider's guided tour of the Graceland of my soul and I pray that you have been moved by what you've seen.

Now comes the hard part. Why did I become a writer? I wrote to say something. I wrote to keep my sanity. I wrote for the oppressed and the downtrodden. I wrote because I couldn't do anything else and I loathe manual labor, but most important: I wrote for Millie, my wife. She was the great love of my life. Seven years ago last week she passed away and since that day, I have not written anything except my letters to you. There were times when I felt like writing, but every time I'd try, I would look over at her empty chair and a sadness, a cruel, incapacitating melancholia would envelop me and bring on the viselike grip of creative paralysis.

Your letters have helped me through this deep, dark despondency and for that I will be eternally grateful. Now I feel beyond sadness and lethargy. I am tired of sleeping alone, of living with ghosts and death, of teaching Spielberg-wannabee clones who have never seen a film made prior to *Star Wars* and want to write only to line their filthy little pockets. You have shown me that there are still a few real writers left, people who write because they have to, they need to, they want to. People who love language and words, who love the way sounds flutter over their tongues and pop out of their lips, the way sentences smell and adverbs taste. I know you feel this way and that is why I have always written back to you.

Never lose your love of language and it will take you far. As for me, I miss my wife. I miss the smell of her suede jacket on rainy afternoons, the way she would brush her index fingers against her lips as she thought, the sound of her spoon tapping against the inside of her coffee mug as she read the newspaper, her tomato sauce—lots of basil, light on the oregano, fresh tomatoes, never canned. I miss feeling her fingers curling the hairs on the back of my neck as we watched movies together. I miss the sound the brass buttons of her jeans made as they turned around and around in our dryer, the flip-flop of her black fuzzy slippers as she walked to the john in the morning, her second smile—that crease between her upper lip and nose—her faint laughter, the little love notes she would leave around the house for me, the tender caresses under the dinner table that no one else could see, her presence at all my lectures, always sitting in the back row, last seat on the right.

Yes, the presence of another who knew me and understood that what I wanted was nothing more than what we all want—to be loved without being judged. And that is how she made me feel for thirty-two years. Even though she is gone, I feel very lucky to have known her.

You ask, if I were younger, and I could do it all over again, what would I want most? And I can think of only one good answer: to meet my wife all over again. To once again feel what it was like to fall in love with her. To be with her and have another thirty-two years together—that would be the best wish of all. But it is only a wish and so now, as I futz around the house, alone, cold, creaky, I feel that without her, there is nothing left to live for. For there is nothing more pathetic than a cranky old grouch.

As for your P.S. about your big pitch at that major production company, I reckon all I can tell you is know your story cold, including the major beats in all three acts, be sensitive to the way those who are listening react to what you are saying, and above all else, have fun. Yes, enjoy it, and the people you are pitching to may enjoy it, too.

Bona Fortuna,

Ra, the Sun God

3/2/04

Dearest Ra-Ra-Ra:

Sorry, I haven't written back sooner, but my life's been crazy. First of all I'd just like to say, thanks to all your advice, help, loving-kindness, and lots of my own innate stubbornness, the people at the production company have bought my movie. Yep. Serious dollars! Major moola. YAHOO! The pitch went great and then I surprised the hell out of them when I whipped out my screenplay and told them it was finished. Then bam! They swooped it up and claim they are sure the people at Fox are going to green-light it and make it.

I'm so freakin' excited! It's the greatest feeling in the world. I can't wait to go back home and sit in the back of my local movie theater and watch everyone watching my movie. And then, wherever I go for the rest of my life, I can stop in a local video store and rent my movie. Mine. The one I wrote. The story that came out of my heart, head, and soul. My characters. The ones that I dreamed up. With your help, of course.

Thank you so much. Kisses. *Besos.* I love you. You are the best. I couldn't have done it without you. I want to take you to Spago for dinner. I want you to go with me to the premiere. Please say yes.

I will always be indebted to you,

I remain sincerely thankful,

Your Favorite Professional Writer

P.S. I know you don't think it's necessary that we ever meet in person, but I couldn't resist. So, I went to the USC campus to find you, but you weren't around. Sorry we missed each other. I guess we'll meet next time I fly to L.A. or definitely at the big premiere.

3/10/04

My Favorite Professional:

Please don't think that I'm dodging you. The truth is I would love to have dinner with you one of these days, but unfortunately, I'm a bit under the weather and have been sticking close to my home. I hope that by the time of your premiere, I will be feeling better.

Regretfully yours and with all my love,

Prof. K.

3/19/04

Dear Prof. K.:

I'm sorry to hear that you're not feeling well.

I wish I were going to be in town so that I could see you, but I regret to say the asswipe suits are bringing in someone else, someone with more credits who is a "known quantity," to rewrite my freaking screenplay. I don't know what this means about the true value of my work, but it don't feel good. The worst part of it all is that I'm out a few hundred thousand dollars and I can't even imagine how many other deals I would have gotten if this stupid project hadn't fallen through. Aaaaargh!

I hate the goddamn city of L.A. and all the goddamn people who live in it (except you, of course). The whole thing is so demoralizing; it's as if I now truly know what the writer in *The Player* felt like when he wanted to kill the studio executive. My problem is I just can't decide whether to kill one of them or if it's easier to just kill myself. Can't wait to hear your response.

As always,

I remain,

Pissed Off

3/23/04

Dear Player:

It happens. But instead of being pissed off, you need to learn to float in the Pacific. Hollywood is not designed to ensure your happiness. It is not set up to give you a sense of your own self-worth or financial security. It is a town where you must hurl your scripts at people until they stick and then, if you're lucky, one day people will start hurling scripts back at you. The only way you ever know if you've made it is when you're no longer hurling, but being hurled at.

No matter what stage of the hurling game you're at, realize that the asswipe suits (as you call them) are scared, insecure people who have to operate in a tainted system that clouds the genius of personal vision with the glaucoma of so-called collaboration. In other words, my dear, let it go.

Think of it this way: Do you expect a thank-you note when you clean your cat's litter box? Do you expect barks of appreciation when you pick up after your dog? Do you get bubbles of graciousness from your goldfish after you feed it? Of course not! Nor should you expect riches or a perfect response to your work. If you spend your life hung up on money and external validation, you will end up hanging yourself. So again, let it go.

Enough moaning and groaning. Keep the faith and above all else, keep writing.

As always,

I remain,

Your Loving Mentor

P.S. Now, it looks as if your true education is really beginning. So, keep fighting the good fight, and don't let me down; I expect very big things from you.

3/28/04

Dear Loving Mentor:

Thank you so much for being my friend and mentor. Now more than ever, I love you and feel very lucky to have your moral support and kind words. You know, thinking back, I can't believe I ever wanted to be a rich and famous writer.

Last week I was so low that I wanted to throw myself into the Pacific. But that seemed to take too much effort. So I stayed in bed for three days in a row, with the curtains drawn, and I wept. My script was my life, my baby, my soul, and I shared it with people who chewed it up and spit it back out in my face!

At the end of the three days, I felt so lonely that all I could do was just hug myself. Yes, I'm embarrassed to say it, but I held myself and rocked back and forth until the sadness seemed to lift. I don't know if I will ever write again, but at least I am finally out of bed and walking around.

Best,

Friend of Dr. Kevorkian

P.S. I guess I am by nature a control freak and the idea of letting go of my work and watching others bastardize it strikes me as incredibly unappealing. In other words, I know I should let go of this project and all the misery involved, but part of me still wants to fight it, get an ulcer, whip out my AK-47, and mow down the bastards. Is this natural?

4/3/04

Dear Youth in Asia,

Yes, it is natural, but it is all just a test.

Let me put everything in perspective. Start by thinking about the nature of work in this market-driven society known as America. Most people have a job to pay the rent. When the rent is paid, the TV comes on and the heavy sedation begins. Like poorly drawn characters in a bad sitcom, there is no growth. Every week, the people remain the same. And even if there is slight growth one week, by the following week, they have reverted back to their original state. Yet you, as one of the exceptional ones, have a calling which allows you to transcend sitcom stupor and experience spiritual growth.

The test begins.

Will the constant rejection destroy you and force you to give up writing? How can you use what happens to you to build you up, and not let it break you down?

The test continues.

Yes, you are cursed with consciousness, so turn the curse into a blessing by using your consciousness to grow and effect positive change in the lives of yourself and others. Think of screenwriting as America's newest spiritual quest. Explore the effects of rejection on the evolution of your personal character. We all fail. We all have some successes. But only a small portion of us is constantly growing, learning, and finding happiness in our lives. Let screenwriting be your greatest guru.

The test never ends.

Jung said, "To be depressed is to be too high up in one's mind." So listen to *The Price Is Right*'s Bob Barker, and come on down.

Get off your self-important pedestal and live a little. Feel your pain and get over it. Like the ancient mariner in Coleridge's great rime, realize that the only way to rid yourself of the albatross hanging from your neck is to love and revere all things that God put in this world, including rejection.

So, live a life of love, not anger. That is all.

I remain,

Your Proctor

P.S. In a letter a few years back, I mentioned the Hollywood Ten. I wasn't one of them, but I was brought up before the House Un-American Activities committee and tail-gunner Joe McCarthy. After refusing to name names, I feel as if I passed my test, and now it is your turn. Don't give in to the pressure; maintain your integrity even if it means having to teach for the rest of your life and never being able to write professionally again. In the end, getting your movies made does not matter, but keeping your soul intact does. Fight to the death for the preservation of your conscience and never name names. Amen!

4/9/04

Dear Proctor K.:

I PASSED THE TEST.

You're not going to believe this, but guess what? After reading your letter, I thought back to the notes the asswipe suits gave me on how to rewrite my script before they hired that other guy. Upon rereading them, I decided to try a few of their suggestions. I did a little bit of a rewrite, not following every single one of their points, but adhering to many of them as well as adding a few new touches of my own for good measure. Then, I sent off the newly revised draft to them. And BAM! I'm back on the project. WHOOPEE! The suits loved the rewrite, canned the script-doctor guy and I'm back on the project. Yippee! I love L.A.!

Oh yeah, please disregard everything I said about Hollywood, the studio system, and the so-called asswipe suits that work there. And don't forget, we've still got a date for dinner and the premiere.

Hugs and kisses,

Your best student ever

P.S. I didn't know you were involved in the era of the Hollywood Ten. Your whole career makes more sense to me now. I'm sorry for all that you must have had to go through and you can rest assured that I'll learn from your experience.

P.P.S. I called USC to try to find out what days you are on campus so I could come by and visit, but the secretary said you've taken ill and are no longer teaching there. Talk to me, what's going on?

4/15/04

Dearest Best Student Ever:

I'm very happy for you. I wish you well and pray that the rest of your Hollywood experiences will be positive ones.

As for my absence from teaching, I have taken some time off because I still don't feel like myself. I guess when you get to be my age, it takes a little longer to get well, but I trust that I will be back at USC soon.

Again, all the best,

Your biggest fan ever

4/21/04

Dearest Biggest Fan Ever:

I'm really sorry about the way you're feeling. Is there anything I can do for you? Please, tell me.

I wish I had good news which might make you feel better, but all I have is bad news. It doesn't look like we'll be going to any premiere because there's a whole new cadre of asswipe suits at the studio now and they've decided to shelve my project and focus on others. Yes, as they say in Tinseltown, we're in turnaround. It looks bleak. I hate everybody and everything in this town. I can't take this roller-coaster ride any longer. Stop the motors, I want to get off. Worst of all, I can't write anymore. Uuuuuuuuhhhhh! All I feel like doing is screaming and destroying things!

HELP!

4/27/04

Dearest HELP!:

I'm sorry this is happening to you, but I am also glad. For it is a gift. I'm sure you do not see it as one right now, but sometimes you need to look below the surface to see what's really going on. This searching will force you to reevaluate the nature of your writing, your life, and your soul. In other words, your wish has been granted; you're finally making money as a professional writer. So, how the hell does it feel, huh?

All the shit you're going through right now can only make you a better writer and a stronger person. Don't fret; just find the blessing in this curse. I've seen the sparks in your smiling prose and I know you can rise above the fray. Your gifts are solid and your soul is strong and true. Obey its voice and rise above the herd.

The interesting thing is—the choices you make now might be even more important than those that you made as a struggling artist. So let's start at the beginning again. Who are you writing for? Why are you writing and what does it all mean in the end? Is it just a job? If you are one of the lucky ones who can write full time, are you really cut out for that kind of life? Do you need another job where you aren't alone all day?

Your next script has to be better than the last. What direction do you want to take with it?

Like our characters, we are all shaped by the choices we make. And in the end, we shall all be judged not by how much money we sell our writing for, but what we do after we make the money. I'm not talking about charity, although that's a very nice gesture. I'm talking about the basic question: Are you still writing? What kind of projects are you writing? What kind of person are you becoming? For when all is said and done, you cannot control how your movie will come out; but if you grow, if you learn, if you change as a result of the process, it is all worthwhile.

So before you slip back into the eternal child, let me leave you with a few more tidbits of wisdom. First of all, everything you need to know about life, you can learn by living, reading great writing, and writing well. That is all and that is everything.

When your big premiere happens—and trust me, if you don't give up and you keep writing, one day it will—what will you do the next morning, especially if the reviews are nasty? Keep in mind that getting produced and going to a screening are merely a blink of the eye, a few hours of your life and then, snap, it'll all be over and you're in for a great fall if you don't have any plans for the after-party. Most of life never lives up to one's expectations. Like the hard-working college student who looks around at his or her graduation ceremony and says, "What the hell do I do now? For years, I couldn't wait to graduate, and now what?"

In the end, it is the writing itself which must suffice, for the shower of sparks falling from your ascending star is ephemeral, but the legacy of your writing can leave a bright light that burns eternally.

Always then, you must continue to work and grow. Your greatest pleasures must come not from rubbing shoulders with celebrities, but from creating a great twist, a wonderful character, or a fantastic climax. You must live in the writing itself, not in the heat of a spotlight that will scorch you soon enough.

I hope that now you finally have some perspective on who we both are and the nature of our shared soul. Do you now see why I've become what I am?

Look closely at me and yourself; acknowledge that nothing is as it first appears.

: Sixteen Little Gifts

The Lakota Sioux Indians judged the greatness of people not by the extent of their accumulated wealth, but by the magnitude of their gift-giving. So I want to give to you, my friend, the greatest gift I can think of. I hope it keeps you through the long nights, the bad reviews, the endless rewrites, and the questioning of self and skill. I hope it does the trick when most of the other answers no longer seem adequate . . .

: 1. We Are All Screenwriters

We are all creative individuals. We are all artists. Poets. The nature of language is inherently symbolic, representative. The letters p-a-p-e-r are not equal to the glorious white stock I am now writing on. The word paper is merely a metaphor, a symbol of the real object which we have come to know as paper. Thus, we live in a world of metaphors, a never-ending swirl of poetry. Embrace the poetic. Never lose your love for the lavender sweet smell of nouns and the salty crunch of adverbs.

: 2. Keep Rewriting

Most of us don't get things right the first time around; don't fret, you can rewrite your life as many times as you need to until you're happy with it. Like your main characters, you always need to be growing, changing, developing. So, don't fear change, embrace it. Be like the Flying Wallendas—a family of trapeze artists who performed all over the world without a net. Fathers and daughters, mothers and sons, always there to protect each other. To catch each other, to support each other. Like the Wallendas, you need a family, some type of writing group or circle of friends who will be there to support you if you start to fall. Armed with this support, stop hanging around the water cooler, go out there, and walk the tightrope of life without a net. Do not fear challenges; instead, fear safety, security, and stagnation.

The question that then inevitably arises is, how do I go about becoming an official Flying Wallenda? The answer is simple. First, keep your mind wide open. Most of the evil in the world originates from ignorance and narrow-mindedness. Be broad in your thoughts, be accepting. Be like the reed at the water's edge, bend with the winds, be sensitive to the world, but never let the bums break you. You'll see that if you keep a window open, even on the coldest days of winter, you might get a bit chilly, but if you're freezing, at least you know that you're alive! Right? RIGHT?

: 3. Create the Rules for Your World

As a writer, you can write anything, as long as you clarify and fully understand the rules of the world that you create. In real life, the rules are already set, but the more fully you understand them, the better chance you have of bending, shaping, and altering them to fit your own needs.

: 4. Don't Give Up, No Matter How Many Drafts It Takes

Yes. Life is hard. Sometimes things don't go your way. Don't pull a Menendez and blow away your parents. Let it go, Eric. Move on, Lyle. Start a new project. Keep writing. You are a writer and no one can take that away from you.

: 5. Enjoy Writing a Good Sentence or Scene

Take pleasure in the simple things and small moments in life. Remember, so-called progress is not necessarily a positive thing and all technology is not inherently good. Yes, you can always e-mail or fax someone, but how about walking over and interfacing, whoops—I mean, conversing with a real live person face to face? Yes, I know it sounds weird, but talking has been a successful means of communication for thousands of years.

: 6. Floss

: 7. Don't Forget to Throw in a Little Comedy

Life is hard and there's already more than enough drama and tragedy in most people's daily existence. So, try to make people laugh and always be willing to laugh at yourself. Believe me, if you've ever really looked at yourself, you have to admit, you're pretty funny looking. And did you know, it's been scientifically proven that laughter will make you live longer? So, as Steve Martin said, "Be thankful for laughter except when milk comes out of your nose."

: 8. The Audience Must Care for Your Main Character and That Only Happens If You Care

In life as in your art, try to be compassionate. Forgive others and, more important, forgive yourself. Life is too short to go through it angry. Try to overlook the faults and negative traits of others. Yes, other people are flawed and insecure, but so are you. Get a new hobby, Lee Harvey, and move on. Meanwhile, rejoice in the passion and beauty of others.

: 9. Never Look Down Upon Others—Whether They Are Fictional Characters or Real People

Do not judge people based upon their profession and/or social class. Find the humanity in everyone. Treat people as if they all have something to offer and what you may find out is that many of them do. Smile a lot at strangers and see how it freaks them out.

After you've asked someone how they are, take the time to listen to their response. Talk to your waiter, your pharmacist, your supermarket checker-outer person. When you speak to them, make eye contact and treat them with respect.

:   10. Don't Hand Over Your Script Too Soon

I know it's tempting, but you only get one chance to make a first impression, so make it a lasting and positive one. Especially in the film business where your script will be covered and labeled forever, no matter how many times you rewrite it. So, don't rush important things. Take your time. Beware of settling for second best. Beware of settling down. Settling in. Settling for. Beware of settling. Resist our conformist market-driven American pack culture mentality that suffocates the creative instincts and diversity of unique individuals. Don't run with the wolves if you were meant to stroll with the great Galapagos turtles or fly with the falcons.

:   11. Expect to Fail

Yes, once you have waited a certain period of time, you will have to hand your script over to other people (see #10), and there is a good chance that it will be rejected. That's okay. Go ahead. Fail. Yes, you heard me, fail! Take the chance and be prepared to fail. It's okay. Happens to the best of us. The only thing that differentiates winners and losers is that after they fail, losers give up and winners try again and again and again. Ted Williams, maybe the greatest baseball hitter of all time, had a batting average of slightly over 400 during his finest season. This, one of the greatest achievements in all of sports history, means that six out of ten times that he got up to the plate, he failed to get a hit. HE FAILED! He failed more than half the time and this failure comes from a man whose batting average was the highest ever. So remember, there will be times when you fail and you are rejected—both personally and professionally. Don't worry, bubbele! A little rejection is good for the soul. Embrace rejection. Use it to push yourself to achieve greater things. Remember, there are no wrong choices. Failures are merely learning experiences that help us to get where we need to go.

: 12. What You Write Can and Will Have
    Ramifications

Be careful of stereotypes, false characterizations, and clichés. Always be aware of the ramifications of your actions and take responsibility for them. As our society grows more and more bizarre, there is a natural tendency to turn inward. Resist it.

: 13. If a Scene or a Line Feels False, Weird, or
    Wrong, It Probably Is

So, when in doubt, don't, whether that means removing a scene that you fear might not propel the story forward or removing someone from your life who is not furthering your growth. We live in a godless age of moral relativism, but God's a pretty smart cookie and knew that even though she gave us a brain that we could use to argue her out of existence, she also implanted in us a little computer-chip conscience that works with or without a deity present. So if something feels wrong, it probably is. Don't do it.

: 14. Take the Business Seriously, for No Matter
    How Artistic You Are, It Is Still a Business

Nature abhors a vacuum and so there are very few vacuums left today, especially good ones. Hence, there is no room in this world for artists to live in vacuums. You are part of a world that is bigger than your own head and social circle. Deal with it. Stay grounded in a pragmatic world view, BUT—and this is a big

BUT—realism breeds mediocrity, and I urge you not toward mediocrity but toward greatness. There is a place for realism, but ask anyone who's ever achieved anything of value and they'll tell you to forget the naysayers who are always screaming "No you can't" and listen to Sammy Davis Jr.'s smoky baritone voice in your heart which sings out, "Yes I can. YES I CAN!"

: **15. Never Lecture and Beware of People Who Give Advice**

: **16. In the End, Your Characters Are Determined by the Choices They Make, Just as You Are Determined by the Choices You Make**

Thus, you and your characters must both make choices which force growth. Expect very few things, but dream of everything. Don't forget to keep that window in your mind open and then, when you become an official Flying Wallenda, you'll never have to look down, you'll never need a net, because you'll be flying through life held aloft by the memory of a professor who loved you.

Zey gezunt.

As always I remain,

Your teacher

5/4/04

Dearest Teach:

Thanks, your letter really helped. And yes, I am learning to find pleasure in writing a good scene or line of dialogue. I am enjoying watching my growth as I engage in revisions and start new projects. I am paying more heed to the process and am becoming less focused on the end result. In other words, I feel lucky to be working as a professional writer.

I think this is important to stress because I never want to become like one of those well-paid Hollywood actors on talk shows who bellyache about how hard their lives are now that they are well-known celebrities. So, yes, I know, at times, being a creative soul can be hard, but I am grateful for the chance to be living a writer's life.

So, every day, I write. Sometimes I get paid. One day, I might even get produced. Maybe I'll be lauded and maybe I'll be denigrated, but either way, I'm a working writer. I send my stuff out there and I go home and write some more. I do what I need to do for my own sanity and happiness. I care about what others think, but I'm no longer a slave to their opinions, because no matter what they say, I can go back to my computer and when I sit, I am safe and happy doing what I do best. I write, I have the moon in my window, and that is enough.

Feel better,

Your Little Zen Monk

P.S. Thanks for all your advice about not putting too much pressure on myself. I know one day, one of my movies will get made and when that happens, I know what I'll do—I'll celebrate with you, and when our celebration is over, I'll go home and write some more.

5/10/04

Dearest Monkey:

I'm so happy to see that you, like all of my favorite characters on the screen, have a true arc. Yes, my little one, it looks like you are finally growing up. It makes me glow with pride. Keep it up, kiddo.

With love,

Professor K.

P.S. I would write more or even fly out to visit, but I'm still not feeling any better.

5/19/04

Dear Prof. K.:

I'm really getting worried now. Are you okay? Why are you not getting any better? What are you suffering from? Is there anything I can do?

For years I've been writing to you at this address and I've never stopped by because I've always respected your privacy, but I really think I should come by when I'm back in L.A. next week. Is this okay?

I want to make sure you are getting my letters. I'm going to be there for some meetings and I'd really love to see you. I make a mean chicken soup. We're talking matzoh balls the size of small children. Please, talk to me. I want to be there for you the way you've been there for me.

Get well soon. And guess what, a big producer who has an office on the Paramount lot is interested in my new script, *Floating in the Pacific*. So, who knows, maybe this one will be the one that gets made. And then again, maybe not; but that's okay too.

Best fishes,

The Flavor of the Week

6/2/04

Dear Rocky Road:

Would have written back sooner, but still a bit sniffly. Thank you so much for your kind words, but I don't want you to have to worry about me or waste your time stopping by my humble abode. I'm doing fine. Right now you need to be focusing on your writing. This is an important time for you. What happens to you over the next few years will make all the difference. Don't waste time worrying about a cranky old fart. Remember what they say about what you should do if you see the Buddha on the road: Kill him, kill him, kill him.

So get out of your little soup kitchen and get your ass back in front of your computer. Write, and that will be the best medicine you could ever give me.

If you feel blocked, look out at the sky or a blade of grass and remember what Gerard Manley Hopkins said: "The world is charged with the grandeur of God, it will flare out like shining from shook foil." So let your words *flare out like shining from shook foil.*

Most important, while all this is happening to you, enjoy it. Savor every goddamn moment. It is the best time of your career. A time of hope and great expectations. All lies ahead and your future looks so bright, I feel like I ought to wear sunglasses. If I can't make it to the premiere with you, I insist that you take someone else. At my age, I don't like to make long-term plans, especially with the Grim Reaper lurking so close. But I've reached a sort of reconciliation with my own mortality. I miss my Millie something awful and so the idea of death seems to me now to be a comforting thing. If we are all born to die, death becomes not a thing to dread, but a democratic concept, universal, an equal opportunity employer.

The hero myth which drives Western culture and films needs to be reevaluated. True courage and real character are found not in how we stand but in how we fall, and what we leave behind after our fall. Let me illustrate with one last film reference. Do you remember the end of *Toy Story?* I'm referring to the moment when Buzz Lightyear glides downward, seeming to be flying, really flying, his lifelong dream achieved for the first time, and his pal Woody screams, "Buzz, you're flying!"

Buzz demurs, "I'm not flying, I'm falling—with style."

Buzz demonstrates that we really can't fly, even if there are times when we may give the appearance of full-fledged flight. Perpetual flight is impossible; we always need to come down to Earth to refuel. It is inevitable. Flight is merely a trick of the light. True, soaring and gliding are possible, but eventually, we all return to the ground, we are all drawn back to Earth, always falling, down, down until there is nowhere else to go; you stop and there is nothing. Nothing. Falling happens.

Thus, we shall always end up being judged not by how we soar through the ozone but by how we land, and what kind of skidmarks we've left on the runway. So, my dear friend, when you fall, fall with style and grace, for all you have left is your fall. And even if you stumble, never be ashamed of trying.

I hope that something of what I say is valuable to you and that you will take some of my words to heart. I have no family and no written record of who I really was—this person whom you have come to know over the course of these letters. The Hollywood films I scripted and the Broadway plays I wrote were commercial vehicles that cannot approximate the amorphous shape of my soul. These letters, then, will have to suffice as the most accurate map of my heart and soul. They are the closest thing I have to a legacy. Take them as my most heartfelt offering and if my thoughts reverberate with you, teach them to your own students. Like ripe, wild boysenberries on a warm summer day, pick them, place them in a chilled porcelain bowl, cover them with real whipped cream, pop them in your mouth, bite down hard, and feel the juice spray against the insides of your cheeks. They are my gift. And if some of the seeds get stuck in your teeth, pick them out, plant them in the ground and watch them grow, for there is no greater pleasure.

Remember then, the only thing that separates good writing from mediocre writing is that good writing has, at its core and in its heart, *love*. Good writers can never sneer at their creations, their characters, their children; like any mother, all you can really do for your children is love them. There is no room in this world for authors who look down their aquiline noses at their characters; forego the disdain, dear heart, and embrace your characters, love them, no matter how evil or despicable they may turn out to be. Write with your pen dipped in the inkwell of compassion, and if you do, you too will always be loved. That is all . . .

And that is more than enough.

Zey gezunt,

Professor K.

P.S. Elie Weisel tells the story of a rabbi in Eastern Europe whose people had a major crisis. They turned to him, their leader, and asked him for help. So the rabbi sat down in a meadow outside his little village, lit a fire, and said a special prayer to the Lord. And as a result of this, his town and all its people were healed.

In the next generation, another crisis occurred and the townspeople now approached the rabbi's son, who did the same as his father. He went out to the meadow. He did not know the prayer or how to light the fire as his father did, but he prayed, and *voila*, the town's problems were healed.

In the following generation, another crisis occurred and the rabbi's grandson wanted to help, but he didn't even know which meadow to go to, although he did know the story of his grandfather, and you know what? That was enough.

Yes, God made human beings to tell stories. So don't ever stop telling your stories . . . and mine.

6/09/04

Dear Professor K.:

Your last letter sounded more like a last will and testament than a friendly epistle and frankly, I'm goddamn worried. I really want to come over and cheer you up. I promise I'll call first. Just tell me it's okay.

Even though we don't have anything tangible to celebrate right now, can't we make something up like good writers often do and have a great big vegetarian dinner? What do you think? Talk to me.

Deeply concerned,

Your dear heart

6/19/04

Dear Professor K.:

Hello? I'm really starting to get crazy now. This isn't like you. I wish you were listed in the phone book or had e-mail or there was some way I could get in touch with you. It's been ten days and I haven't heard a thing.

I'm convinced something is wrong. Call me. Write me. I'm going nuts here. I want to see you. I want to make sure you are okay. I want to see if there is anything I can do to help. Why won't you let me see you? You mean so much to me.

Hurry,

Overwrought

Afterword

The following is the text of the eulogy delivered at the memorial service for Professor Abraham Krevolin at the University of Southern California Hillel Center, 29, June 2004.

Dear Friends and Students of Professor Abe Krevolin:

For the next few minutes, I will try to do my best to express to you how I felt about Professor Abe Krevolin. First of all, I'd just like to assure everyone here today that Prof. K.'s dog, Meshugeneh, is fine and living with me now. Also, please excuse me, I'm a writer, not an actor, so I'm not used to doing this kind of thing, especially in front of so many people. And, well, revealing my emotions has never been my forte. But I'd like to try to do justice to a man who changed my life. Ours was an unconventional relationship, based on a love of language, writing, movies, and theater. In fact, we never met face to face.

Regardless, I feel fortunate to have been able to know Professor K. through his letters. Oh, how I loved his letters! Every day, I couldn't wait to get to my mailbox to see if he had written to me. His letters were things of beauty filled with dark fire and raw electricity. Words—beautiful, strong, melodic words—swirled off his pages. I was transfixed. Invigorated. Transformed by his thoughts and lessons. He reached out to me and touched me when I thought no one could. He patted me on the back and caressed my cheeks. He told me I was going to be okay, converted me back into a human being. He made me believe that I counted, that I was worthwhile, good, and important. I wanted to stay in the presence of his letters forever.

Yes, I admit it—over the course of our correspondence, I fell in love with my professor, but who wouldn't fall in love with someone who brings a few rays of love and light into this world of darkness and hatred; who wouldn't rejoice in the purity of souls touching and connecting?

For over six years, we sent letters back and forth. I trace my growth by the path of these letters, and I attribute everything I have achieved as a writer to his tutelage. And now, today, I want to tell you a little bit about the legacy that Prof. K. left me.

Prof. K. and I spoke of change as being the primary factor in a successful story, but Prof. K. taught me that it is not merely change or courage, it is more; it is obsession and beyond. Yes, all great stories have one thing in common: characters who are driven beyond obsession, who love more deeply than us ordinary folks, who fight harder, and hold on longer. Characters who are beyond obsession shed light on our lives, they teach us how to live, inspire us to be extraordinary, to transcend the security of narrow-mindedness, and to always and forever strive to become better.

After years of receiving loving guidance from Prof. K., I see today as my first chance to start giving something back, to help Abe finally finish reaping the fruits that he planted. But exactly how would Prof. K want me to do this? And then, I thought of the legends and myths of other cultures that we would discuss, especially those of the Lakota Sioux Indians, who judged the greatness of others not by the extent of their accumulated wealth, but by the magnitude of their gift-giving.

So as we now say good-bye to Prof. K., I want to give back to you the greatest gift I can think of: Prof. K.'s blessing. I was fortunate to have had Prof. K.'s blessing bestowed upon me and I want to share with you. Prof. K. always made me feel safe, gifted, and proud to be his student and a writer. Now I would like to extend his blessing to all of you . . .

FLOATING IN THE PACIFIC—AN ELEGY

There are no more rewrites to do.
There are no books left to read,
no papers left to correct,
no movies left to analyze.
No more letters left to write . . .

You struggled your whole life,
to be heard, to effect change,
to write a perfect sentence
and now it's time to rest.
You deserve it.
Zey gezunt, Abe.

For the greatest gift you can give
is your blessing
and you blessed us all with your life,
you words,
your thoughts,
your wisdom,
your kindness,
and your love.

And so now, in return, take a small gift from us,
receive our blessing—

Zey gezunt, Abraham.
Because of you
we will never stop writing,
we will never stop trying to effect change,
we will never settle for anything less.

We will always keep our minds open,
our eyes clear and our voices pure.

Whenever a good story is well told,
we will always hear your voice in our own.
When we look down at the blank page,
we will always see your handwriting.
Whenever we write a perfect scene,
It will be your advice guiding us,
and when we fall asleep at night and dream,
together
we shall float in the Pacific . . .

6/12/09

Dear Prof. Holt:

I am an aspiring screenwriter who is a big fan of all the films you have written. So I thought you would be the best person to talk to. Do you think I should go to film school or just use the money I would have spent on film school to live as a full-time screenwriter for a few years?

Also, I've heard that you sometimes work as a writing consultant and I would love to have you read my work. How much do you charge?

I would give you all the money I have in the world if you could help make me into a screenwriter. Please help.

Sincerely Yours,

Aspiring Away

P.S. I have included a copy of my most recent screenplay, *When I Grow Up*, which I thought you might be able to peruse at your earliest convenience.

From the Desk of Prof. F.X. Holt, USC Film School

6/23/09

Dear Aspiring:

1. I don't want your filthy money.
2. Keep aspiring.
3. Your screenplay, *When I Grow Up*, is now floating in the Pacific.

Best,

Prof. H.

P.S. What do you want me from me? As a great writer, Abraham Krevolin, once said, "No one can make someone into a real writer. You are either born with the curse or not. The reasons why God chooses to whisper into the ear of one woman and not another are known only to her . . . "

Appendix A: Special Information

From the Desk of Prof. Richard Krevolin

Dear Reader:

Unlike Prof. Abe Krevolin, I'd love to hear from you and can be contacted in writing, c/o Renaissance Books, 5858 Wilshire Boulevard, #200, Los Angeles, CA 90036-4521. Or, you can e-mail me at *krevolin@usc.edu.* Or even visit my Web site, *http://www-rcf.usc.edu/~krevolin.*

Patience, perseverance, and persistence.

Thanks and keep writing,

Hammering Away in Hollywood

Appendix B: Filmography

Air Force One *Director:* Wolfgang Petersen; *writer:* Andrew W.
Marlowe (Buena Vista, 1997)

Apocalypse Now *Director:* Francis Ford Coppola; *writers:*
Michael Herr, John Milius, and Francis Ford Coppola (United
Artists, 1979)

Austin Powers: International Man of Mystery *Director:* Jay
Roach; *writer:* Mike Myers (New Line, 1997)

Back to the Future *Director:* Robert Zemeckis; *writers:* Robert
Zemeckis and Bob Gale (Universal, 1985)

Batman *Director:* Tim Burton; *writers:* Sam Hamm and Warren
Skaaren (Warner Bros., 1989)

Beetlejuice *Director:* Tim Burton; *writers:* Michael McDowell
and Warren Skaaren (Warner Bros., 1988)

Blade Runner *Director:* Ridley Scott; *writers:* Hampton Fancher
and David Peoples (Warner Bros., 1982)

Butch Cassidy and the Sundance Kid *Director:* George Roy Hill;
writer: William Goldman (Twentieth Century-Fox, 1969)

Casablanca *Director:* Michael Curtiz; *writers:* Julius J. Epstein,
Philip G. Epstein, and Howard Koch (Warner Bros., 1942)

Citizen Kane *Director:* Orson Welles; *writers:* Orson Welles and
Herman J. Mankiewicz (RKO, 1941)

Con Air *Director:* Simon West; *writer:* Scott Rosenberg
(Touchstone, 1997)

Dead Presidents *Directors:* Albert Hughes and Allen Hughes;
writers: Michael Henry Brown, Albert Hughes, and Allen
Hughes (Universal, 1994)

Die Hard *Director:* John McTiernan; *writers:* Jeb Stuart and
Steven E. DeSouza (Twentieth Century-Fox, 1988)

Dirty Harry *Director:* Don Siegel; *writers:* Harry Julian Fink, Rita M. Fink, and Dean Riesner (Warner Bros., 1971)

Dog Day Afternoon *Director:* Sidney Lumet; *writer:* Frank Pierson (Warner Bros., 1975)

The English Patient *Director:* Anthony Minghella; *writer:* Anthony Minghella (Miramax, 1996)

Evita *Director:* Alan Parker; *writers:* Alan Parker and Oliver Stone (Hollywood, 1996)

Forrest Gump *Director:* Robert Zemeckis; *writer:* Eric Roth (Paramount, 1994)

Free Willy *Director:* Simon Wincer; *writers:* Keith A. Walker, Corey Blechman, and Tom Benedek (Warner Bros., 1993)

Full Metal Jacket *Director:* Stanley Kubrick; *writers:* Stanley Kubrick and Gustav Hasford (Warner Bros., 1987)

The Glass Menagerie *Director:* Paul Newman; *writer:* Tennessee Williams (Cineplex Odeon, 1987)

Glory *Director:* Edward Zwick; *writer:* Kevin Jarre (Tri-Star, 1989)

The Godfather *Director:* Francis Ford Coppola; *writers:* Francis Ford Coppola and Mario Puzo (Paramount, 1972)

The Godfather Part II *Director:* Francis Ford Coppola; *writers:* Francis Ford Coppola and Mario Puzo (Paramount, 1974)

The Graduate *Director:* Mike Nichols; *writers:* Calder Willingham and Buck Henry (Embassy, 1967)

Heathers *Director:* Michael Lehmann; *writer:* Daniel Waters (New World, 1989)

Hercules *Directors:* John Musker and Ron Clements; *writers:* Irene Mecchi, John Musker, Ron Clements, Bob Shaw, and Donald McEnery (Buena Vista, 1997)

Home Alone *Director:* Chris Columbus; *writer:* John Hughes (Twentieth Century-Fox, 1990)

Home Alone 2: Lost in New York   *Director:* Chris Columbus; *writer:* John Hughes (Twentieth Century-Fox, 1992)

Independence Day   *Director:* Roland Emmerich; *writers:* Dean Devlin and Roland Emmerich (Twentieth Century-Fox, 1996)

In the Heat of the Night   *Director:* Norman Jewison; *writer:* Stirling Silliphant (United Artists, 1967)

Jaws   *Director:* Steven Spielberg; *writers:* Peter Benchley and Carl Gottlieb (Universal, 1975)

The Jazz Singer   *Director:* Alan Crosland; *writers:* Alfred Cohn and Jack Jarmuth (Warner Bros., 1927)

Judge Dredd   *Director:* Danny Cannon; *writers:* William Wisher, Steven E. DeSouza, Michael De Luca, and William Wisher (Buena Vista, 1995)

Jurassic Park   *Director:* Steven Spielberg; *writers:* David Koepp and Michael Crichton (Universal, 1993)

The Lion King   *Directors:* Roger Allers and Robert Minkoff; *writer:* Irene Mecchi (Buena Vista, 1994)

The Lost World: Jurassic Park 2   *Director:* Steven Spielberg; *writer:* David Koepp (Universal, 1997)

Love Streams   *Director:* John Cassavetes; *writers:* Ted Allan and John Cassavetes (MGM, 1984)

Men in Black   *Director:* Barry Sonnenfeld; *writer:* Ed Solomon (Columbia, 1997)

Midnight Cowboy   *Director:* John Schlesinger; *writer:* Waldo Salt (United Artists, 1969)

Mrs. Doubtfire   *Director:* Chris Columbus; *writers:* Randi Mayem Singer and Leslie Dixon (Twentieth Century-Fox, 1993)

Monty Python's Life of Brian   *Director:* Terry Jones; *writers:* John Cleese, Graham Chapman, Terry Gilliam, Eric Idle, Michael Palin, and Terry Jones (Orion, 1979)

Muriel's Wedding *Director:* P. J. Hogan; *writer:* P. J. Hogan (Miramax, 1994)

My Best Friend's Wedding *Director:* P. J. Hogan; *writer:* Ronald Bass (TriStar, 1997)

On the Waterfront *Director:* Elia Kazan; *writer:* Budd Schulberg (Columbia, 1954)

Ordinary People *Director:* Robert Redford; *writer:* Alvin Sargent (Paramount, 1980)

Platoon *Director:* Oliver Stone; *writer:* Oliver Stone (Hemdale, 1986)

The Player *Director:* Robert Altman; *writer:* Michael Tolkin (Fine Line, 1992)

Pretty Woman *Director:* Garry Marshall; *writer:* J. F. Lawton (Touchstone, 1990)

The Producers *Director:* Mel Brooks; *writer:* Mel Brooks (Embassy, 1968)

Psycho *Director:* Alfred Hitchcock; *writer:* Joseph Stefano (Paramount, 1960)

Pulp Fiction *Director:* Quentin Tarantino; *writers:* Quentin Tarantino and Roger Avary (Miramax, 1994)

The Purple Rose of Cairo *Director:* Woody Allen; *writer:* Woody Allen (Orion, 1985)

Quiz Show *Director:* Robert Redford; *writer:* Paul Attanasio (Hollywood Pictures, 1994)

Raging Bull *Director:* Martin Scorsese; *writers:* Paul Schrader and Mardik Martin (United Artists, 1980)

Rambo: First Blood Part II *Director:* George Pan Cosmatos; *writers:* Sylvester Stallone, James Cameron, and Kevin Jarre (Tri-Star, 1985)

Say Anything *Director:* Cameron Crowe; *writer:* Cameron Crowe (Twentieth Century-Fox, 1989)

Scream   *Director:* Wes Craven;   *writer:* Kevin Williamson (Dimension, 1996)

The Seventh Seal   *Director:* Ingmar Bergman;   *writer:* Ingmar Bergman (Svensk, 1957)

Shine   *Director:* Scott Hicks;   *writer:* Jan Sardi (Fine Line, 1996)

Sixteen Candles   *Director:* John Hughes;   *writer:* John Hughes (Universal, 1984)

Sleepless in Seattle   *Director:* Nora Ephron;   *writers:* Nora Ephron, David S. Ward, and Jeff Arch (Columbia, 1993)

Sling Blade   *Director:* Billy Bob Thornton;   *writer:* Billy Bob Thornton (Miramax, 1996)

Speed   *Director:* Jan DeBont;   *writer:* Graham Yost (Twentieth Century-Fox, 1994)

Splash   *Director:* Ron Howard;   *writers:* Lowell Ganz, Babaloo Mandel, and Bruce Jay Friedman (Touchstone, 1984)

Stand by Me   *Director:* Rob Reiner;   *writers:* Raynold Gideon and Bruce A. Evans (Columbia, 1986)

Stargate   *Director:* Roland Emmerich;   *writers:* Dean Devlin and Roland Emmerich (MGM, 1994)

Star Trek—The Motion Picture   *Director:* Robert Wise;   *writers:* Harold Livingston and Alan Dean Foster (Paramount, 1979)

Star Wars   *Director:* George Lucas;   *writer:* George Lucas (Twentieth Century-Fox, 1977)

Sullivan's Travels   *Director:* Preston Sturges;   *writer:* Preston Sturges (Paramount, 1941)

Sunset Boulevard   *Director:* Billy Wilder;   *writers:* Billy Wilder, Charles Brackett, and D. M. Marshman Jr. (Paramount, 1950)

The Terminator   *Director:* James Cameron;   *writers:* James Cameron and Gale Anne Hurd (Orion, 1984)

Terms of Endearment   *Director:* James L. Brooks;   *writer:* James L. Brooks (Paramount, 1983)

Thelma & Louise   *Director:* Ridley Scott; *writer:* Callie Khouri (MGM, 1991)

To Kill a Mockingbird   *Director:* Robert Mulligan; *writer:* Horton Foote (Universal, 1962)

Top Gun   *Director:* Tony Scott; *writers:* Jim Cash and Jack Epps Jr. (Paramount, 1986)

Toy Story   *Director:* John Lasseter; *writers:* Joss Whedon, Andrew Stanton, Joel Cohen, Alec Sokolow, John Lasseter, Pete Docter, and Joe Ranft (Buena Vista, 1995)

2001: A Space Odyssey   *Director:* Stanley Kubrick; *writers:* Stanley Kubrick and Arthur C. Clarke (MGM, 1968)

Under Siege   *Director:* Andrew Davis; *writer:* J. F. Lawton (Warner Bros., 1992)

Waiting to Exhale   *Director:* Forest Whitaker; *writer:* Ronald Bass (Twentieth Century-Fox, 1995)

Wayne's World   *Director:* Penelope Spheeris; *writers:* Mike Myers, Bonnie Turner, and Terry Turner (Paramount, 1992)

Welcome to the Dollhouse   *Director:* Todd Solondz; *writer:* Todd Solondz (Sony Classics, 1995)

When Harry Met Sally . . .   *Director:* Rob Reiner; *writer:* Nora Ephron (Columbia, 1989)

The Wizard of Oz   *Directors:* Victor Fleming and King Vidor; *writers:* Noel Langley, Florence Ryerson, and Edgar Allan Woolf (MGM, 1939)

Young Guns   *Director:* Christopher Cain; *writer:* John Fusco (Twentieth Century-Fox, 1988)

Bibliography

Ackerman, Diane. *A Natural History of Love.* New York: Vintage Books, 1995.

_____. *A Natural History of the Senses.* New York: Vintage Books, 1990.

Allen, Woody. *Without Feathers.* New York: Ballantine Books, 1990.

Aristotle. *Poetics.* Trans. by Gerald F. Else. Ann Arbor, Mich.: The University of Michigan Press, 1967.

Brooks, Peter. *Reading for the Plot: Design and Intention in Narrative.* Cambridge: Harvard University Press, 1992.

Bukowski, Charles. *Run with the Hunted: A Charles Bukowski Reader, John Martin, Ed.* New York: HarperPerennial, 1994.

DeLillo, Don. *White Noise.* New York: Penguin USA, 1991.

Dillard, Annie. *The Writing Life.* New York: HarperCollins, 1990.

Egri, Lajos. *Art of Dramatic Writing.* New York: Simon & Schuster, 1977.

Frankl, Viktor E. *Man's Search for Meaning.* New York: Washington Square Press, 1997.

Field, Syd. *Screenplay.* New York: Fine Communications, 1998.

Freud, Sigmund. *Beyond the Pleasure Principle.* New York: W. W. Norton, 1990.

Gardner, John. *The Art of Fiction: Notes on Craft for Young Writers.* New York: Vintage Books, 1991.

_____. *On Moral Fiction.* New York: Basic Books, 1979.

Goddard, Harold C. *The Meaning of Shakespeare Vols. 1 and 2.* Chicago: University of Chicago Press, 1960.

Hauge, Michael. *Writing Screenplays That Sell.* New York: HarperPerennial, 1991.

Hillman, James. *The Soul's Code: In Search of Character and Calling.* New York: Warner Books, 1997.

Howard, David and Edward Mabley. *The Tools of Screenwriting: A Writer's Guide to the Craft and Elements of a Screenplay.* New York: St. Martin's Press, 1995.

Keen, Sam. *To a Dancing God.* San Francisco: HarperCollins, 1990.

Lamott, Anne. *Bird by Bird: Some Instructions on Writing and Life.* New York: Anchor, 1995.

Lawson, John Howard. *Theory and Technique of Playwriting and Screenwriting.* New York: Garland, 1985.

Ludwig, Arnold. *The Price of Greatness: Resolving the Creativity and Madness Controversy.* New York: The Guilford Press, 1996.

Mast, Gerald and Marshall Cohen. *Film Theory and Criticism: Introductory Readings.* New York: Oxford University Press, 1992.

Ray, Robert Beverley. *A Certain Tendency of the Hollywood Cinema.* Princeton, N.J.: Princeton University Press, 1985.

Rilke, Rainer Maria. *Letters to a Young Poet.* Trans. by Stephen Mitchell. New York: Vintage, 1987.

Seger, Linda. *Making a Good Script Great.* New York: Samuel French, 1994.

Sturges, Preston. *Five Screenplays.* Ed. by Brian Henderson. Berkeley, Calif.: University of California Press, 1986.

Vogler, Christopher. *The Writer's Journey: Mythic Structure for Storytellers and Screenwriters.* Studio City, Calif.: Michael Wiese Productions, 1992.

Walter, Richard. *Screenwriting: The Art, Craft, and Business of Film and Television Writing.* New York: New American Library, 1992.

Wright, Will. *Sixguns and Society.* Berkeley, Calif.: University of California Press, 1977.

Index

About the Author

Richard Krevolin is a screenwriter, playwright, poet, and professor. A graduate of Yale University, Richard earned a master's degree in screenwriting at UCLA's School of Cinema-Television and a master's degree in playwriting and fiction from USC's Professional Writing Program.

Among Richard's accomplishments are his screenplays *Trotsky's Garden, Maternal Instincts, The Pride of Wartburg, Hoops, Overtime,* and *One Mo' River,* which are all in different stages of development. He was a finalist for the $500,000 Kingman Screenwriting Award and the Nicholl Screenwriting Fellowship. His one-man play, *Yahrzeit,* a finalist in the HBO New Writer's Project, ran at the Santa Monica Playhouse for five sold-out months; under a new name, *Boychik,* it opened Off-Broadway at Theatre Four in New York City in 1997, and is now touring the country. He is the author of *The Delancey Trilogy,* a series of three one-man shows that include *Seltzer Man, Second Banana!,* and *The Law of Return (The Meyer Lansky Story),* which won the Seventh Annual Streisand Festival of New Jewish Plays and has been performed in Chicago, New York, New Haven, and Los Angeles. He received a Valley Theatre League nomination for best director and best play for his one-man musical *RebbeSoul-O,* which is being performed all over the country.

Besides his talents as a writer, Richard has been motivating and inspiring students through his teaching at USC in the School of Cinema/TV since 1988. He has also taught at Pepperdine University, the University of Redlands, and Los Angeles Community College, and now conducts writing seminars and private workshops. For more information, contact him at *krevolin@usc.edu.*